The New England Table

The New England Table

by LORA BRODY

photographs by SUSIE CUSHNER

CHRONICLE BOOKS

SAN FRANCISCO

Library of Congress Cataloging-in-Publication Data available.

ISBN 0-8118-4349-1
MANUFACTURED IN CHINA.

Prop styling by HELEN CROWTHER
Food styling by JEE LEVIN
Designed by VANESSA DINA
Typesetting by BLUE FRIDAY

PHOTOGRAPHER'S ACKNOWLEDGMENTS:
The good will and generosity that was offered to me throughout the past nine months of shooting this project has been overwhelming. It clearly reflects the genuine good nature and spirit of New Englanders. I wish to thank Jonathan Singer for inviting us to join him at Fenway Park; Bob Hampson for guiding us through the beautiful cranberry bogs; Barbara Lauterbach for hosting us during the Ice Fishing Derby; Corey Family, Peter Purington, Ann Branon and her nephews, Evan Branon, Michael James Angelino, and John Luc Landry for sharing the magic of maple sugaring; Hilary Maslow for providing a cozy home base for all the Vermont locations; David Chamutka for teaching us how to harvest fiddleheads; and Bud Gallie for trusting his instincts and inviting us into his authentic Maine home as a location for many of the finished food shots. The success of this book is owed in great part to the experience, talent, and hard work and creativity of Helen Crowther; the effortless food styling of Jee Levin; and assistance from Margaret Matyia. My sincere gratitude to Aleta Robison and Tasney Mazzarino for keeping the budget and production in check, and to Owen Cortet and Jenna and Kayla Cushner for unconditional love and patience. All these people have truly been the force behind this creation. Finally, my thanks to the author, Lora Brody, for giving me the opportunity to experience New England, my home region, in a more expansive way than I ever have.

DISTRIBUTED IN CANADA BY RAINCOAST BOOKS
9050 SHAUGHNESSY STREET
VANCOUVER, BC V6P 6E5

10 9 8 7 6 5 4 3 2 1

CHRONICLE BOOKS LLC
85 SECOND STREET
SAN FRANCISCO, CALIFORNIA 94105

www.chroniclebooks.com

Dedication:

IN LOVING MEMORY OF JULIA CHILD AND LESLIE REVSIN

***

Acknowledgments:

Once again I rejoice in the opportunity to express my gratitude to the team of
talented, dedicated, patient, and determined women who work with me in the kitchen as
well as at the keyboard. Emmy Clausing both tested dishes and made sure that
every 'i' was dotted and every 't' was crossed in each recipe and headnote I wrote.
Susan Schwartz created and tested recipes, exhibiting her usual cheerful energy
and downright refusal to settle for anything less than perfect.

I am grateful to freelance food writer Cheryl Sternman Rule, who also did a terrific job of
testing recipes. Barbara Lauterbach and Tom Wilson were perfect hosts at an unforgettable
weekend at the annual Ice Fishing Derby in Center Harbor, New Hampshire.
The following people graciously allowed me to use their recipes: Barbara Lauterbach,
Kathy Gunst, Diana Dunn, and Dr. Leo Salzman.

Thank you to Judith Ellen Johnson of the Connecticut Historical Society for
information about the Nutmeg State, and to Bob Hanson for the opportunity to
photograph the cranberry harvest in Massachusetts.

The beautiful photographs in this book were the result of the talent and
hard work of Susie Cushner, Helen Crowther, and Jee Levin.

A special thank you to my muse, PJ Hamel, who got me jump-started on this
project and was never farther away than the nearest phone when I needed help.

Never-ending gratitude goes to my Super Agent, Susan Ginsburg, who,
just as I hand in one manuscript, wants to know 'What's next?'

How many writers can say emails to their publisher end in GO SOX? My editor,
Amy Treadwell, may live on the West Coast, but her devotion to the Red Sox just about matches
mine. I found it a special thrill to receive the galleys for this book on the day the Sox beat
the New York Yankees for the American League Pennant. The fact that the Sox went on to win
the World Series will keep both of us smiling until Opening Day, 2005.

FENWAY FRANKS, CODFISH CAKES, CONCORD GRAPES, LOBSTER BISQUE, MAPLE SYRUP, ISLAND LAMB, DAY-BOAT SCALLOPS: THE BUFFET THAT THE NEW ENGLAND STATES LAY OUT FOR THE ENJOYMENT OF ITS CITIZENS AND VISITORS ALIKE IS SUMPTUOUS AND IDIOSYNCRATIC. IN THE KITCHEN, THE POT IS STIRRED BY THE LIKES OF FANNIE FARMER, JULIA CHILD, AND MARK TWAIN. DAIRY FARMS AND FIELDS OF SWEET CORN; PEACH AND APPLE ORCHARDS; THE BOUTIQUE VINEYARDS; AND FORESTS TEEMING WITH GAME CONTRIBUTE INGREDIENTS TO STOCK NEW ENGLAND'S PANTRY. THE LARDER OVERFLOWS WITH THE CATCH OF THE ATLANTIC SHORELINE. SEEING HOW EACH STATE'S TRADITIONS TURN THIS NATIVE BOUNTY INTO MEALS BOTH FESTIVE AND FAMILIAR IS CAUSE FOR CELEBRATION WITH EVERY COURSE.

Small in scale and fiercely independent, each New England state, along with pride in regional likenesses, works hard to maintain its own unique character and personality. Culinary distinctions are no exception. New Englanders know that spring has arrived when roe from Connecticut River shad appears in fish stores; if the weather holds there will be native sweet corn for Fourth of July; and there's a restaurant in Portland, Maine, that serves Elk Osso Buco.

Like a slow but determined diner with a ravenous appetite pressing towards the table, the Laurentide glacier moved south from Canada, scouring and

sculpturing land that the Pilgrims called New England. The crop of the fieldstones and boulders it planted became the bane of every farmer who attempted to till the often flinty, sometimes fertile soil. Dug and hauled by hand, this inedible harvest became the building blocks of the stone walls that to this day divide and define the area made up of Connecticut, Massachusetts, Rhode Island, New Hampshire, Vermont, and Maine. Looking like a patchwork quilt rich in texture and color, these walls, frugal and practical just like their builders, mirror the New England character. Fitted together without the benefit of mortar, each stone, distinct yet supporting its neighbor, represents an essential part of the whole. Inwardly fractious, outwardly solid, the rough, seemingly barren New England landscape supports all manner of living things.

Imagine blueberry coffee cake for breakfast in Bar Harbor; a lunch of lobster salad in Conway, New Hampshire, followed by a maple-pecan ice cream cone at a back-road Vermont creamery; a tea party in Boston; deep-dish pizza in Providence; and a nightcap in Greenwich, Connecticut. It is physically possible to dine in each New England state in the course of one long day. Nevertheless, sites and attractions, from the capricious and often violent weather of New Hampshire's Mount Washington to the glint of sunlight bouncing off hulls of Newport's million-dollar yachts, as well as the distinctive culinary culture of each state, make a long visit and many meals in New England a worthy goal.

Connecticut, the contented matron—complete with a single strand of pearls, a smoked salmon canapé, and a finishing school education—digs her toes into the sands of Long Island Sound and entertains with elegantly refined menus. The Nutmeg State is a comforting blend of farms and small cities connected by large tracts of Main Street, U.S.A. suburbia.

The warm-water coastline, bisected by the mouth of New England's perhaps most beloved river, the Connecticut, leads eventually to Rhode Island, a brazen little state, simmering with a heady stew of old-line Yankee, Portuguese, and Italian families that looks for all the world like it shouldered itself into a tiny gap between Connecticut and Massachusetts. In Rhode Island, all roads lead to Providence, the state's capital, largest city, and epicenter. On the way through, stop for a slaw dog and a "cabinet" (milk shake) to fortify you for making your way through the tangle of highways that slash through Providence. Farther east, the state borders Massachusetts's southern coast, and acts as a sentry for Cape Cod.

Massachusetts, a state of contrasts—beaches, dunes, lush green meadows, and the shadowy blue hills of its western Berkshire mountains—is where the Pilgrims stepped ashore at Plymouth Rock nearly four hundred years ago. Ever since, the door has been open and the world has poured in. Thai, San Salvadoran, Puerto Rican, East and West African, Korean, Hmong, and Vietnamese cooks present old-to-them, new-to-us ingredients and flavors, jousting and blending with staid Yankee fare. The results are at times spectacular, resulting in dishes like fried oysters with kaffir lime, cilantro, and lemongrass mayonnaise on restaurant menus.

Vermont and New Hampshire, alter egos divided by the upper reaches of the Connecticut River, perch side by side above Massachusetts. While Vermont, with its softly rolling meadows and benign Green Mountains, has long based its economy on dairy farming (it's no accident that it's the home state of Ben and Jerry's ice cream), New Hampshire's granite-streaked soil gave rise to roaring rivers used to power the mills that turned the southern half of the state into a manufacturing mecca. Up north, New England's tallest mountains, the Whites, anchor a small wilderness of streams and forests, a hiker's paradise that provides the Appalachian Trail's most majestic views. From Mount Washington, at 6,288 feet—New England's highest peak and home to the "world's worst weather"—you can look east and see Maine, the giant thumbprint-shaped state that serves as New England's far northeast border.

Maine is a land of lobstermen and potato farmers, sailors and shopkeepers, writers, woodsmen, and fishing fanatics. It is also the land of blueberry pie, oyster festivals, and bumper stickers that caution you to "Brake for Moose—It Could Save Your Life." Maine has more millionaires per capita than any other state; it's also ranked at or near the bottom, nationwide, in per capita income. Though all of the rest of New England could fit inside Maine's borders, the vast majority of Mainers cluster close to her 3,500 miles of rocky shoreline, which torques and twists through bays, islands, and inlets, plotting an intricate path from Kittery to Eastport. Inland, hardier souls live at the edges of the Great North Woods, an area so vast that it's simply divided into numbered, rectangular plots so that its timber cutters and log haulers won't get lost.

New England is one of the smallest geographically and culturally distinct areas of America, yet the bounty of its table is vast and varied. We natives proudly boast of unique culinary traditions: making steaming pots of Indian pudding to take the chill off howling blizzards; spreading elaborate picnics on open tailgates in college football stadium parking lots or in forests lit by fireworks of fall foliage; savoring the smoky sweetness of newly made maple syrup poured over snow; and foraging for fiddlehead ferns and dandelion greens at the first sight of spring. Every season brings its own delights to our kitchens, giving us endless reasons to fire up the oven and call family and friends to the table.

Massachusetts

Bring your appetite to the state that hosted not only the first Thanksgiving, but the nation's first tea party as well. Start your meal with authentic **New England Corn and Clam Chowder** (the kind without tomatoes), and end it with a dish of warm **Indian Pudding** topped with a scoop of vanilla ice cream. Save room in between for a helping of **Boston Baked Beans** and, if you are lucky enough to take in a baseball game, a **Fenway Frank** or two. You may have to run the **Boston Marathon** to keep in shape as you savor the culinary delights of the **Bay State**.

AFTER A HIKE ON THE ROCK-STREWN SHORE,
YOU'LL BE READY TO DIG INTO THIS HEARTY BREAKFAST
STARRING ONE OF MASSACHUSETTS'S BEST-LOVED INGREDIENTS:
GARNET-HUED CRANBERRIES.

cranberry-orange spritzers

cranberry-pecan hotcakes with caramel-rum sauce

firecracker bacon

applejack baked apples with ricotta cream

cranberry-orange spritzers

***

SERVES 8

**These refreshing drinks are
as beautiful as a tropical sunset and
available much closer to home.**

To make the ice-cube garnish, select two ice cube trays; pour the
orange juice into one and the cranberry juice into the other. Freeze
until solid.

To make the spritzers, pour ½ cup of freshly squeezed orange juice
into each of eight 12-ounce glasses. Add ½ cup of cranberry juice to
each glass and then ¼ cup of sparkling water. Add several cranberry
and orange ice cubes to each, garnish with a sprig of fresh mint, if
desired, and serve immediately.

For the ice-cube garnish:

1 cup (8 ounces) commercially
prepared, pulp-free orange juice

1 cup (8 ounces) cranberry juice

For the spritzers:

1 quart (32 ounces) freshly
squeezed orange juice

1 quart (32 ounces) cranberry juice

2 cups (16 ounces) sparkling water,
cranberry-flavored if possible

Fresh mint sprigs (optional)

cranberry-pecan hotcakes with caramel-rum sauce

***

MAKES ABOUT 15 HOTCAKES

**With a breakfast like this, you may find yourself
fully sated right up to supper time. Both the sauce and batter
(without the addition of the pecans and cranberries)
can be prepared the night before and
stored in a covered container in the refrigerator.
Just before making the hotcakes, gently stir in the nuts and
berries. If you have made the sauce ahead of time,
reheat it before serving.**

For the Caramel-Rum Sauce:

2 cups (16 ounces) granulated sugar

1 cup (8 ounces) water

1 tablespoon fresh lemon juice

4 tablespoons (½ stick; 2 ounces) unsalted butter, cut into several pieces

½ cup (4 ounces) heavy cream

⅓ cup (3 ounces) dark rum (optional)

1 tablespoon pure vanilla extract

For the hotcakes:

½ cup (2 ounces) cranberries, fresh or frozen

½ cup (2 ounces) pecans

3 tablespoons granulated sugar

1 cup (5 ounces) unbleached all-purpose flour

½ teaspoon salt

½ teaspoon baking powder

½ teaspoon baking soda

½ teaspoon ground cinnamon

1 cup (8 ounces) plain yogurt

2 extra-large eggs

⅓ cup (2.67 ounces) whole milk

¼ teaspoon pure vanilla extract

4 tablespoons (½ stick; 2 ounces) unsalted butter

To make the caramel sauce, place the sugar, water, and lemon juice in a heavy-bottomed 2-quart saucepan. Place over high heat and stir just until the sugar dissolves and the mixture is clear. Bring the syrup to a rapid boil, then cook without stirring until the syrup turns a deep amber color, 12 to 15 minutes. Do not let the syrup burn. Remove it from the heat and stir in the butter, bit by bit, then add the cream, rum (if using), and vanilla. Set aside and let cool slightly. (Leftover sauce will keep, refrigerated, for up to 1 week.)

To make the hotcakes, place the cranberries, pecans, and sugar in the work bowl of a food processor and pulse until the mixture is finely chopped. Sift the flour, salt, baking powder, baking soda, and cinnamon into a medium bowl. In a large bowl, whisk together the yogurt, eggs, milk, and vanilla. Add the flour mixture to the egg mixture and beat together until very well combined. Fold in the cranberry mixture.

Heat a large griddle or nonstick skillet over medium heat and grease it well with 2 tablespoons of the butter, reserving the rest to regrease the pan for the subsequent hotcakes, if necessary.

Drop the batter by ¼-cup portions onto the hot griddle or skillet and cook for 2 to 3 minutes, until the bottoms are well browned. Flip the pancakes and cook for another 2 minutes, adjusting the heat as necessary to be sure the pancakes don't burn, until the second side is well browned and the centers are cooked. Serve immediately with the warm Caramel-Rum Sauce. You can keep the cooked pancakes warm in a single layer on a baking sheet, covered with foil, in a 200°F oven.

firecracker bacon

***

MAKES 12 SLICES

The inspiration for this recipe came from Diana Dunn, who used it as part of her final creative project in culinary school. Thank you, Diana! The combination of sweet and spicy is irresistible; you'll find yourself sampling often even before the serving dish hits the table. Feel free to decrease the amount of cayenne pepper if you prefer less of a kick.

½ cup (4 ounces) firmly packed dark brown sugar

½ teaspoon cayenne pepper

12 slices thick-cut bacon

Preheat the oven to 425°F with the rack in the center position. Line a rimmed baking sheet with aluminum foil. Select a rectangular cooling or roasting rack that can fit on the baking sheet, spray it with non-stick cooking spray, and place it on the foil-lined baking sheet.

In a small bowl, stir together the brown sugar and cayenne pepper. Place the bacon slices side by side on the prepared rack and, using your hands or a rubber spatula, rub the mixture onto the top of each bacon slice. Press gently to be sure the mixture adheres. Don't be concerned if a small amount of the mixture falls between the grates of the rack. Bake the bacon for about 20 minutes, or until it is cooked through and quite crisp. Be prepared for the oven to be a bit smoky when you retrieve the bacon. Place the baking sheet on a second wire rack, transfer the bacon to a plate, and serve hot.

The bacon can be cooked up to a day ahead, refrigerated, then reheated in the microwave oven in a microwave-safe dish lined with several sheets of paper towel. Place a layer of paper towels on top of the bacon as well to keep the microwave clean.

applejack baked apples with ricotta cream

***

SERVES 6

For the Ricotta Cream:

1 cup (8 ounces) ricotta cheese

¼ cup (2 ounces) granulated sugar

1 tablespoon heavy cream

1 tablespoon orange-flavored liqueur such as Grand Marnier

6 large, firm apples, such as Gravenstein, Ida Red, or Northern Spy

¾ cup (3 ounces) dried cranberries

⅔ cup (5.5 ounces) chopped almonds

½ cup (4 ounces) firmly packed brown sugar

2 tablespoons (1 ounce) unsalted butter, at room temperature

½ cup (4 ounces) plus 1 tablespoon applejack or other apple brandy

Baked apples is a dessert that conjures up thoughts of other comfort foods such as macaroni and cheese and tomato soup. Some of the rather nontraditional ingredients in this version make it a tad more sophisticated while keeping it as homey as can be. If you wish, you can substitute apple cider or even orange juice for the brandy called for below.

To make the Ricotta Cream, place the ricotta cheese, granulated sugar, heavy cream, and liqueur in a small bowl and mix well until well blended and smooth. Refrigerate until ready to use. The Ricotta Cream may be made up to a day ahead.

Preheat the oven to 350°F with the rack in the center position. Wash the apples well and use a paring knife or grapefruit knife to core the apples. Scoop out enough of the center to leave a 1-inch space that does not extend through the bottom of the apple.

In a small bowl, mix together the dried cranberries, chopped almonds, brown sugar, and butter until well blended. Place 1 tablespoon of the cranberry mixture in the cavity of each apple. Place the apples in a 9-inch ovenproof glass pie plate and pour the ½ cup of applejack around the apples. Add water so that the liquid comes about 1 inch up the sides of the apples. Sprinkle the remaining 1 tablespoon of applejack evenly over the filling in the apples and bake for 25 to 30 minutes, until the apples are tender.

Serve warm or cold, topped with a generous dollop of Ricotta Cream.

TANGLEWOOD PICNIC

THE SUMMER HOME OF THE BOSTON SYMPHONY ORCHESTRA
IS LOCATED IN LENOX, IN THE HEART OF
THE BEAUTIFUL BERKSHIRE HILLS. THE TRADITION HERE
IS TO COME EARLY, SPREAD YOUR PICNIC BLANKET ON
THE EXPANSIVE LAWN, AND ENJOY YOUR REPAST
UNDER (HOPEFULLY) BLUE SKIES. AFTER LUNCH (OR SUPPER)
THE BLANKET BECOMES A PLACE TO LIE DOWN,
CLOSE YOUR EYES, AND ENJOY THE MUSIC.

pimm's cup
page NO. 20

summer fruit salad
page NO. 20

picnic sesame chicken with honey-mustard dipping sauce
page NO. 24

hummus focaccia in honor of yo-yo ma
page NO. 26

double-chocolate coconut cookies
page NO. 30

pimm's cup

¼ cup (2 ounces) Pimm's Cup No. 1

7-Up or ginger ale

1 slice cucumber

Twist of lemon

Pimm's No. 1 is an English liqueur, available in liquor and wine stores. Gin-based, with the addition of spices and fruit juices, the formula, created in the mid-1800s by a pub owner named James Pimm, remains a deep, dark secret. What happened to Pimm's numbers 2, 3, and 4 is a mystery as well. This makes a refreshing, easy-to-make cocktail perfectly suited to an elegant lawn picnic.

Pour the Pimm's into a tall glass filled with ice. Top off with the 7-Up or ginger ale and garnish with the cucumber slice and lemon twist.

summer fruit salad

***

SERVES 8

3 cups pineapple rings (preferably fresh), cut in quarters

1 large, ripe mango, peeled and cut into 1½-inch cubes

1 papaya, peeled, seeded, and cut into 1½-inch cubes

3 kiwis, peeled, quartered, and thickly sliced

2 star fruits, sliced

1 cup (4 ounces) unsweetened shredded coconut

2 slightly underripe bananas, peeled and cut into 1-inch slices

⅓ cup (2.7 ounces) orange juice

Fresh pomegranate seeds (optional)

This finished dish looks like a bowlful of sparkling jewels. It is best to shop several days ahead so that the fruit will be ripe and flavorful.

Put the pineapple, mango, papaya, kiwis, star fruits, coconut, bananas, and orange juice in a large plastic container and mix gently. Sprinkle the pomegranate seeds, if using, on top. Cover and refrigerate or keep cool until ready to serve.

PIMM'S CUP
see page N⁰. 20

SUMMER FRUIT SALAD

see page N°. 21

picnic sesame chicken with honey-mustard dipping sauce

4 whole boneless,
skinless chicken breasts, or
2 pounds chicken tenders

2 teaspoons coarse salt

½ teaspoon freshly ground
black pepper

2 tablespoons toasted sesame oil

¼ cup (2 ounces) vegetable oil

3 tablespoons soy sauce

¼ cup (2 ounces) good-quality
mayonnaise

2 cups (8 ounces) sesame seeds,
lightly toasted (see note)

**For the Honey-Mustard
Dipping Sauce:**

½ cup (4 ounces) Dijon mustard

½ cup (4 ounces) honey

¼ cup (2 ounces) cider vinegar

1 tablespoon fresh lemon juice

½ cup (4 ounces) canola oil

¼ cup (2 ounces) mild olive oil

Freshly ground black pepper

"Wow! Homemade chicken nuggets," exclaimed one of my sons, as I pulled these from the oven. In truth the homemade version with sesame seeds rather than a breaded coating yields much more flavor and a much more interesting and pleasing texture. Served hot or cold, it makes an easy-to-eat appetizer or picnic meal—especially if you are using your fingers in place of a fork.

Wash the chicken and pat it dry. If using whole breasts, cut them crosswise against the grain into 2½-inch strips. Season both sides of the chicken pieces with the salt and pepper. Put the sesame and vegetable oils, soy sauce, and mayonnaise in a small bowl; whisk to combine. Place the chicken and the mayonnaise mixture in a heavy-duty zippered plastic bag or in a glass bowl. Toss or mix to cover all the pieces (if using a bowl, cover with plastic wrap), then refrigerate for at least 1 hour and up to 24 hours.

When ready to cook the chicken, preheat the oven to 425°F with the rack in the upper third (but not highest position) of the oven. Pour the sesame seeds into a clean gallon-size zippered plastic bag. Using a slotted spoon, transfer the chicken pieces from the marinade to the bag with the sesame seeds. Press on the bag lightly and try to coat each piece of chicken completely with seeds. Lay the pieces in one layer on 2 aluminum foil–lined shallow baking dishes or rimmed sheet pans and bake for 20 minutes, or until the chicken is opaque throughout.

Meanwhile, make the dipping sauce: Put the mustard, honey, vinegar, and lemon juice in the work bowl of a food processor and pulse 6 to 8 times to combine well. Slowly add the canola oil and then the olive oil through the feed tube with the processor running. When the sauce has thickened and all the oil is added, add pepper to taste and process to mix well. (To make the sauce by hand, whisk together the mustard, honey, vinegar, and lemon juice in a medium bowl. Add the canola oil and the olive oil in a very thin, steady stream, whisking constantly. Whisk in pepper to taste.) Store the dipping sauce in a covered, nonreactive container for at least 1 hour and up to 24 hours before serving.

Place the chicken under the broiler about 4 inches from the heating element for 1 to 2 minutes or until the seeds on the top are toasted but not burned. Allow the chicken to cool for 10 minutes at room temperature before refrigerating. Serve hot or cold with the Honey-Mustard Dipping Sauce.

NOTE: To toast sesame seeds, line a rimmed baking sheet with paper towels. Put the sesame seeds in a large, dry, heavy skillet set over high heat. Shake the pan briskly back and forth to agitate the seeds, or stir constantly with a wooden spoon, until the seeds turn light golden brown. Transfer immediately to the prepared baking sheet to cool; the seeds will continue to cook briefly, so be careful not to overbrown.

hummus focaccia in honor of yo-yo ma

***

MAKES 1 LARGE LOAF

⅓ cup vegetable oil

2 cloves garlic, smashed

2½ teaspoons active dry yeast

1 tablespoon Lora Brody's Bread Dough Enhancer (optional, for a chewier loaf; see notes)

2 cups (10 ounces) unbleached all-purpose flour

½ cup (2.5 ounces) whole-wheat flour

½ cup (2.5 ounces) toasted chickpea flour (see notes)

1½ teaspoons regular molasses (not blackstrap) or honey

1½ teaspoons salt

⅓ cup (2.7 ounces) sesame seeds, toasted (see notes)

¾ cup (6 ounces) milk

1 cup (8 ounces) prepared hummus

1 extra-large egg

Coarse salt and freshly ground black pepper (optional)

At Christmastime a couple of years ago, I got a frantic call from our local Williams-Sonoma store. "I'm desperate," said the manager. "Yo-Yo Ma is here and wants to buy a copy of your bread machine book, and we're all out. If we give you his address can you send him one?" Could I??!! I signed the book, thanking him for all the pleasure his music had given our family. Almost by return mail I received a CD—a cello sonata in "Sour Do Major," along with a note of thanks.

Several months later, I was catching a very early flight out of Boston. The airport was practically deserted, but it could have been a mob scene and still I would have recognized the handsome man rolling a cello case down the concourse, coming towards me. Even though I love to be recognized by my fans, I would never run up to someone famous just to say hello. Seeing him close up was enough for me. But when he sat down a few seats away and smiled at me briefly as he did, I figured, Hey, we've got some kind of relationship— I mean, he has my book and I have that autographed CD. I screwed up my courage, leaned over, and said, "I want to thank you for the CD you sent me." He looked bemused and quizzical at the same time. "The Mozart sonata in Sour Do Major," I clarified.

"Wow, you're Lora Brody!" He jumped out of his seat. "I think you're just wonderful! That book you wrote with your mother has turned me into a real bread baker." Next thing I knew he was giving me a hug, and I truly thought I had died and gone straight to heaven.

Ever since that day I've been thinking about what kind of bread I might create to dedicate to cellist and bread baker extraordinaire Yo-Yo Ma. And this is what I've come up with. It's a loaf in which the ingredients harmonize and make beautiful music together.

Place the oil and garlic in a glass measure. Cover with plastic wrap and microwave for 30 seconds. Allow to cool before removing the plastic wrap. Remove the garlic and discard. Reserve 3 tablespoons of the garlic oil for brushing on top of the bread before it bakes; the remaining oil will be used in the bread dough.

This dough can be made by hand, with a stand mixer, in a food processor, or in a bread machine.

To make the dough by hand: Put the yeast, Dough Enhancer (if using), all-purpose flour, whole-wheat flour, chickpea flour, molasses, salt, sesame seeds, milk, hummus, egg, and remaining garlic oil in a large mixing bowl and mix until a soft dough begins to form. Turn the dough out onto a lightly floured work surface and knead for 5 to 7 minutes, adding water or all-purpose flour as necessary, until a smooth, elastic dough forms. Return the dough to the mixing bowl and cover the top with plastic wrap. Let the dough rise in a warm place until doubled in bulk. Gently deflate the dough, re-cover the bowl, and refrigerate for at least 4 hours and up to 24 hours.

To make the dough in a stand mixer: Put the yeast, Dough Enhancer (if using), all-purpose flour, whole-wheat flour, chickpea flour, molasses, salt, sesame seeds, milk, hummus, egg, and remaining garlic oil in the bowl of a stand mixer fitted with the dough hook. Knead on low speed until a ball starts to form, then increase the speed to medium and knead for 5 to 7 minutes, adding more all-purpose flour as necessary, until a soft, supple ball of dough forms. Turn off the mixer, remove the dough hook, leave the dough in the bowl, and cover with plastic wrap. Let the dough rise in a warm place until doubled in bulk. Gently deflate the dough, re-cover the bowl, and refrigerate for at least 4 hours and up to 24 hours.

To make the dough in a food processor: Put the yeast, Dough Enhancer (if using), all-purpose flour, whole-wheat flour, chickpea

CONT'D

flour, molasses, salt, sesame seeds, milk, hummus, egg, and remaining garlic oil in the work bowl of a food processor fitted with the dough blade. Pulse on and off for 30 seconds to combine the ingredients into a sticky mass. Process for 40 seconds, then let rest for 5 minutes. Process for 30 seconds more, adding more all-purpose flour as necessary, until a soft, supple ball of dough forms. Transfer the dough to a lightly oiled bowl or a large heavy-duty zippered plastic bag and let rise in a warm place until doubled in bulk, then gently deflate it. Cover the bowl or close the bag, pushing out the air, and refrigerate the dough for at least 4 hours and up to 24 hours.

To make the dough using a bread machine: Put the yeast, Dough Enhancer (if using), all-purpose flour, whole-wheat flour, chickpea flour, molasses, salt, sesame seeds, milk, hummus, egg, and remaining garlic oil in the bread machine and program for Dough or Manual. Allow the machine to go through one knead and one rise. Check during the first few minutes of the first knead cycle and add more all-purpose flour or water as necessary, until a soft, supple ball of dough forms. When the dough has doubled in bulk, transfer the dough to a lightly floured work surface and deflate it gently. Place the dough in a bowl, cover it with plastic wrap, and refrigerate the dough for at least 4 hours and up to 24 hours.

To complete the bread, lightly coat a large, heavy-duty baking sheet with vegetable oil. Remove the dough from the refrigerator and pat it into a 12-inch circle; place it on the prepared baking sheet. Brush the dough with the reserved 3 tablespoons garlic oil and sprinkle lightly with coarse salt and pepper, if desired. Let rise at room temperature, uncovered, until doubled in bulk. When the dough is about halfway risen, preheat the oven to 475°F with the rack in the center position. When doubled in bulk, use your fingertips to quickly dimple the top.

Bake the focaccia until the top is golden brown, 15 to 18 minutes. Let cool before cutting into wedges to serve.

This bread can be made up to 2 days in advance. After cooling, wrap in plastic wrap or aluminum foil and store at room temperature. It can also be frozen for up to 3 months. Defrost at room temperature, still in its wrapping.

NOTE: Lora Brody's Bread Dough Enhancer is available at www.lorabrody.com, 888-9-Bakeit, or at the King Arthur Flour Baker's Catalogue, www.kingarthurflour.com, 800-827-6836.

NOTE: Toasted chickpea flour is available in health-food stores and well-stocked supermarkets.

NOTE: To toast sesame seeds, line a rimmed baking sheet with paper towels. Put the sesame seeds in a large, dry, heavy skillet set over high heat. Shake the pan briskly back and forth to agitate the seeds, or stir constantly with a wooden spoon, until the seeds turn light golden brown. Transfer immediately to the prepared baking sheet to cool; the seeds will continue to cook briefly, so be careful not to overbrown.

double-chocolate coconut cookies

* * *

MAKES ABOUT 30 COOKIES

2 cups (10 ounces) unbleached all-purpose flour

1 teaspoon baking soda

1 teaspoon salt

1 cup (2 sticks; 8 ounces) unsalted butter, at room temperature

⅔ cup (5.4 ounces) firmly packed light brown sugar

⅔ cup (5.4 ounces) granulated sugar

2 extra-large eggs, at room temperature

1 teaspoon pure vanilla extract

¼ teaspoon almond extract

⅔ cup (2 ounces) regular (not Dutch-processed) cocoa powder, sifted

1½ cups (6 ounces) sweetened flaked coconut

1½ cups (7.5 ounces) milk chocolate chips or milk chocolate bars broken or chopped into ¼-inch pieces

These divine and completely irresistible cookies are the brainstorm of my exceptionally talented recipe tester, Cheryl Rule, who loves coconut almost as much as she loves chocolate. The double chocolate in the name refers to the creamy milk chocolate morsels nestled in a chocolate cookie base. If you have a favorite brand of milk chocolate bar, break it into small (¼-inch) pieces and use it in place of the chips.

Preheat the oven to 350°F with 2 racks placed as close to the center of the oven as possible. Line 2 baking sheets with parchment paper or silicone pan liners.

Sift together the flour, baking soda, and salt in a medium bowl; set aside. In the bowl of a stand mixer fitted with the paddle attachment, cream the butter, light brown sugar, and granulated sugar on medium speed until light and fluffy, about 5 minutes. Scrape down the sides of the bowl from time to time as you work. With the mixer running, beat in the eggs one at a time, mixing well until each egg is fully incorporated. Add the vanilla and almond extracts; beat well until combined. Turn the mixer to low speed and gradually add the cocoa powder and the flour mixture and mix gently just until combined. Fold in the coconut and chocolate chips.

Drop the batter by heaping tablespoons onto the prepared baking sheets, allowing about 1½ inches between cookies. (If you have a scale, each portion of dough should weigh approximately 1 ounce.) Bake for 12 to 14 minutes, rotating the baking sheets top to bottom and front to back halfway through for more even baking. The cookies are done when the edges are firm and the centers lose their shine. Do not overbake. Cool on the sheets for about 5 minutes, then transfer the cookies to a wire rack to finish cooling.

These cookies freeze beautifully in a freezer bag. Just thaw them at room temperature until they have softened enough to eat.

FEEDING THOSE MIGHTY BRAVE (OR FOOLISH) INDIVIDUALS
(AND THEIR SUPPORT TEAMS) WHO HAVE OR ARE ABOUT TO RUN
THE 26 MILES, 385 YARDS FROM HOPKINTON TO BOSTON
ON PATRIOT'S DAY (HELD ON OR AROUND APRIL 18TH TO COMMEMORATE
THE START OF THE AMERICAN REVOLUTION) MAY SEEM
A DAUNTING TASK. FEAR NOT, THIS EASY MENU HAS MOSTLY
DO-AHEAD RECIPES THAT WILL PROVIDE ENOUGH SUSTENANCE
TO HOLD THE CREW UNTIL THE NEXT MARATHON.

corn and clam chowder
page №. 32

mediterranean layered salad
page №. 34

boston baked beans
page №. 36

bagged brisket
page №. 38

strawberry whipped cream celebration cake
page №. 42

corn and clam chowder

2 pounds chopped clams, defrosted if previously frozen, with their liquid

4 ears sweet corn, defrosted if frozen, husked if fresh

6 cups (48 ounces) whole milk

3 cups (24 ounces) heavy cream

6 ounces salt pork or smoked bacon, cut into ¼-inch cubes

2 tablespoons (1 ounce) unsalted butter

1 large onion, peeled and cut into small dice

2 stalks celery, with leaves, minced

3 tablespoons unbleached all-purpose flour

3 large Idaho potatoes (about 2½ pounds), peeled and cut into ½-inch cubes

1 tablespoon fresh thyme leaves or 2 teaspoons dried thyme

Salt and freshly ground black pepper

⅓ cup fresh flat-leaf (Italian) parsley leaves, minced

Butter and paprika for garnish

Oyster crackers for serving

Don't ever mention the word *tomatoes* in the same sentence as *clam chowder* to a New Englander. There's New York chowder (thin, watery, with tomatoes), and then there's New England style: hearty, thick with potatoes, and rich with butter and cream. Once you've had the real thing, you'll never consider eating the imposter again.

The unusual step of simmering the corn still on the cob in milk as a base for this hearty chowder gives it a lovely sweet flavor. You can use fresh or frozen ears of corn, found in the supermarket, for this recipe. You can also start by steaming your own clams (see note), but I think buying chopped clams, which are available both fresh and frozen in most supermarkets, is just as good and far, far less work.

Drain the liquid from the clams and set aside. Combine the corn and milk in a large stockpot set over medium-high heat. Cover and bring to a gentle simmer. Cook for 5 minutes, then turn off the heat and let the corn cool for a few minutes in the milk. Remove the corn to a cutting board and let it cool until it can be handled, then remove the kernels by running a sharp knife down the length of the cobs. Separate the kernels and set aside. Return the cobs to the pan with the milk and simmer for 5 more minutes to get as much flavor from them as possible. Use a slotted spoon or tongs to remove the corncobs. Discard the cobs. Add the cream and the clam liquid to the pot and reduce the heat to very low.

Place the salt pork or bacon in a large skillet set over medium-high heat. Cook, stirring frequently and pouring off and discarding any accumulated fat, until crisp, about 15 minutes. Reduce the heat to medium and add the butter. When the butter has melted, add the onion and celery and sauté until soft and slightly golden brown, about 15 minutes. Add the flour and cook, stirring constantly, for 2 to 3 minutes, or until light golden brown. Whisk in 1 cup of the hot milk mixture and then transfer the contents of the skillet to the pot with the remaining hot milk mixture. Whisk to combine.

Raise the heat under the milk mixture and bring to a gentle simmer. Add the potatoes and cook until just tender, 15 to 20 minutes. Add the clams, corn kernels, and thyme. Bring the chowder to a gentle simmer and cook just until heated throughout, about 2 minutes. Season with salt and pepper to taste and ladle into warmed bowls. Sprinkle with the parsley and top each with a pat of butter and a dusting of paprika. Pass the oyster crackers at the table.

NOTE: If you are using fresh clams, you'll need about 9 pounds. Place the clams and 2 cups of water in a large stockpot set over high heat. Cover, bring to a simmer, and cook until the clams open, about 4 minutes. Use a slotted spoon to remove the clams to a bowl, discarding those that have not opened. Strain the cooking liquid through a fine-mesh or cheesecloth-lined sieve and reserve. Take the clams out of their shells and chop them into ½-inch pieces.

mediterranean layered salad

4 cups (32 ounces) plain
whole-milk yogurt

1 medium eggplant (about 1 pound),
peeled and cut into 1-inch cubes

3 tablespoons extra-virgin olive oil

1 teaspoon salt

1 cup (8 ounces) prepared hummus

One 20-ounce jar roasted
red peppers, drained

1 cup (4 ounces) crumbled
feta cheese

1 cup (5 ounces) drained, pitted
Kalamata olives, coarsely chopped

¼ cup fresh flat-leaf (Italian) parsley,
coarsely chopped

**This is a dual-purpose dish that you can serve
either as an appetizer dip with chips or pita wedges or
as a salad course. All the best flavors and textures
of the Mediterranean meet and meld together to make
for a lovely presentation and an even better taste.**

**Begin making this recipe several hours (or a day) ahead
to give the yogurt time to drain and release its liquid.
This will thicken the yogurt and prevent it
from leaking into the other layers of the salad.**

Line a large sieve with two layers of cheesecloth or paper towels. Place the sieve over a deep bowl and spoon the yogurt into the lined sieve. Cover with plastic wrap, pressing it onto the surface of the yogurt, and allow to drain in the refrigerator for several hours or overnight.

Have ready a 5-cup glass serving bowl. (Using a glass bowl is important so you can see the beautiful layers in the salad.)

Preheat the oven to 400°F with the rack in the center position. Place the eggplant in a single layer on a rimmed baking sheet lined with aluminum foil. Drizzle on the olive oil and sprinkle with the salt. Use your hands or a slotted spoon to toss the eggplant, coating it evenly with oil and salt. Roast the eggplant until tender, about 25 minutes, stirring with a wooden spoon about halfway through the cooking time. Remove from the oven and allow to cool to lukewarm. Put the eggplant in the work bowl of a food processor fitted with the metal blade and pulse until thickly puréed. Transfer the eggplant to the serving bowl and smooth the top with a rubber spatula.

Remove the drained yogurt from the refrigerator; discard the liquid in the bowl. Spread the yogurt on top of the eggplant. Smooth the top gently with a clean rubber spatula. Carefully spread the hummus, again with a clean rubber spatula, on top of the yogurt and smooth the top. Be careful not to press down too hard or the layers will intermingle, disturbing the visual effect.

Clean and dry the food processor. If the roasted red peppers were packed in vinegar, rinse them and pat them dry. Otherwise, just pat them dry and purée them in the food processor. They won't be completely smooth, which is fine. Transfer the peppers to a cheesecloth-lined sieve and press down on them with a spoon for several minutes to extract as much liquid as possible. Gather up the corners of the cheesecloth and lift the purée out of the sieve. Twist the corners together to extract any remaining liquid. (The more liquid you can remove the better.) Spread the red pepper purée on top of the hummus and smooth the surface with a clean rubber spatula. Sprinkle the crumbled feta evenly over the red pepper purée. Scatter the olives over the feta. Top with the chopped parsley. Cover the bowl with plastic wrap and refrigerate for at least 1 hour and up to 24 hours before serving.

boston baked beans

* * *

SERVES 6 TO 8 AS A MAIN COURSE OR 10 TO 12 AS A SIDE DISH

1 pound (16 ounces) dried kidney beans, rinsed and picked over for stones or dirt

1 regular or smoked ham bone, or ½ pound thick-sliced bacon, cut into 1-inch pieces

2 large onions, peeled and cut into ¼-inch dice

½ cup (4 ounces) firmly packed brown sugar

¼ cup regular molasses (not blackstrap)

1½ teaspoons dry mustard

1 teaspoon salt

1 teaspoon ground ginger

¼ teaspoon dried sage

I love any chance to quote Julia Child, who lived in Cambridge, Massachusetts, for many years before she moved to California. We offer her method of par-boiling the beans in this recipe to get out the "root-e-toots." Unlike the speedy runners that might be destined to eat this dish, slow and easy is the byword here. The longer this dish simmers, either in a bean pot, heavy casserole dish, or slow cooker, the better it will taste.

Put the beans in a large pot with water to cover by 4 inches and bring to a boil over high heat. Boil for 2 minutes, then remove the pot from the heat, cover the pot, and allow the beans to sit in the hot water for 1 hour. Drain the beans and transfer them to a large, ovenproof, covered casserole; to a bean pot; or to the insert of a slow cooker. If you are using a casserole or bean pot, preheat the oven to 225°F. If you are using a slow cooker, use the low setting. Add to the beans 6 cups of fresh water, the ham bone or bacon, onions, brown sugar, molasses, mustard, salt, ginger, and sage; mix well. Cover and cook for 8 hours in the oven or slow cooker. (You can also cook the beans on the stove top in a large, heavy-bottomed, covered pot. Combine the drained beans, 6 cups fresh water, and the remaining ingredients in the pot and bring to a boil over medium-high heat, then reduce the heat to its lowest setting and cook for 6 hours.) Stir the beans occasionally (whether in the oven or on the stove top) to be sure they aren't drying out or in danger of burning. If so, add 1 cup boiling water and stir well. The beans are done when they are softened and the sauce is thick and dark brown.

At this point, the beans can be cooled and refrigerated for several days. To reheat them, add 1 cup of water before warming in a 325°F oven or on the stove top over low heat for at least 1 hour. Stir the beans occasionally as they heat.

bagged brisket

***

SERVES 6

5 to 6 pounds first-cut brisket

2 large onions, peeled and thickly sliced

4 stalks celery, with leaves, cut into ½-inch slices

4 thick carrots, peeled and cut into ½-inch rounds

One 12-ounce can beer

One 8-ounce bottle chili sauce

4 cloves garlic, peeled and minced

2 bay leaves

½ cup (4 ounces) water

½ cup (4 ounces) firmly packed dark brown sugar

⅓ cup (2.7 ounces) Dijon mustard

¼ cup (2 ounces) red wine vinegar

¼ cup (2 ounces) regular molasses (not blackstrap)

¼ cup (2 ounces) soy sauce

1 teaspoon paprika

Salt and freshly ground black pepper

Don't be put off by the number of ingredients here— this recipe has just a few steps, it's easy to make, and it's well worth it. A great place to find this special cut of meat is a kosher meat market, although any grocery store with a meat department should be able to order one for you.

Oven roasting bags can be found in the aluminum-foil section of the supermarket. You want the "turkey-size" bag for this recipe.

Preheat the oven to 300°F with the rack in the lower third (but not the very bottom position) of the oven. Place a heavy-duty sauté pan or skillet over high heat, add the brisket, and sear the meat on both sides until browned. Discard any fat. Place a large oven roasting bag (see recipe introduction) in a roasting pan. Place the brisket in the bag. Scatter the onions, celery, and carrots over the meat.

Put the beer, chili sauce, garlic, bay leaves, water, brown sugar, mustard, vinegar, molasses, soy sauce, and paprika in a large mixing bowl and whisk to combine. Pour the liquid into the bag with the brisket, press out the air, and use a twist tie to seal the top. Use the tip of a sharp knife to cut several small slits near the closure so that air can escape. Bake for 4 hours. The brisket won't suffer if you cook it for up to another hour—in fact, it just becomes more tender and flavorful.

Carefully cut open the bag and transfer the brisket to a cutting board. Strain the cooking liquid into a saucepan, reserving the vegetables. If you have time, chill the liquid and remove the hardened fat. Otherwise, skim off and discard as much of the fat as possible with a large metal spoon. Season the cooking liquid with salt and pepper to taste. Return the vegetables to the liquid and reheat gently.

Use a long, sharp knife to cut the meat against the grain into thin slices. Arrange the slices on a rimmed serving platter. Distribute the vegetables around the meat and pour the cooking liquid over the meat before serving.

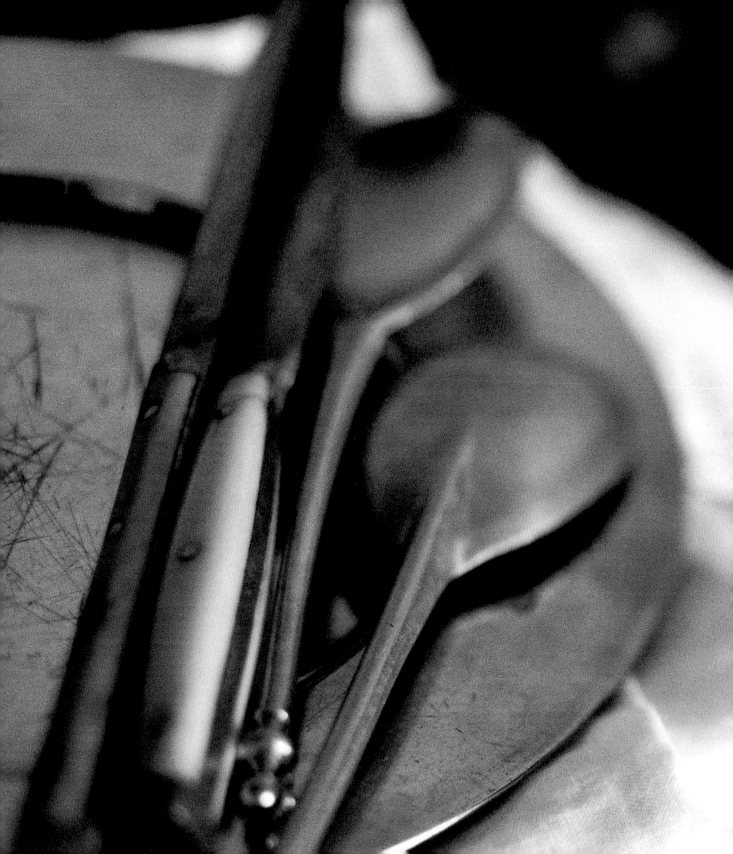

BOSTON BAKED BEANS

see page N°. 36

STRAWBERRY WHIPPED CREAM CELEBRATION CAKE
see page №. 42

strawberry whipped cream celebration cake

2½ cups (12.5 ounces) unbleached all-purpose flour

1½ cups (12 ounces) granulated sugar

½ teaspoon salt

2½ teaspoons baking powder

¾ cup (6 ounces) whole milk

4 extra-large eggs

2 teaspoons almond extract

1 cup (2 sticks; 8 ounces) unsalted butter, chilled and cut into 8 pieces

⅔ cup (7 ounces) lemon curd (see note)

2 pints fresh strawberries, hulled, rinsed only if necessary and gently patted dry (we've left some green leaves on a few whole berries on top for added color)

1 cup (8 ounces) heavy cream, whipped to soft peaks with 2 tablespoons confectioners' sugar and 1 teaspoon almond extract

This cake itself is a reason to celebrate, and, if you make it to honor someone who has achieved approaching the completion of a marathon, you will be right smack in the winner's circle and guaranteed an invitation to next year's post-race festivities (as long as you promise to bring the cake, that is). Two golden layers sandwiched with tangy lemon curd and fresh strawberries, crowned with whipped cream— it's gorgeous to behold and extraordinary to taste. There won't be a single crumb left over.

Preheat the oven to 350°F with the rack in the center position. Butter the bottom and sides of two 9-inch round cake pans and line the bottoms with circles of parchment paper. Butter the parchment, then dust with a little flour; knock out the excess.

In a large mixing bowl or the bowl of a stand mixer, sift together the flour, sugar, salt, and baking powder; set aside. Whisk together the milk, eggs, and almond extract in a spouted measuring cup or small bowl. Set aside.

Scatter the butter pieces over the flour mixture and cut the butter into the flour mixture using two butter knives or a pastry blender until the lumps are the size of peas. Add half of the milk mixture. Using a handheld or stand mixer set on low speed, beat for 5 to 10 seconds, then increase the speed to high and beat for 1 minute. Scrape down the sides of the bowl as you work. Add the remaining milk mixture and continue to beat on high speed until the batter is thick and smooth. Pour and scrape the batter into the prepared pans, and smooth the tops with a rubber spatula.

Place the pans at least 2 inches apart on the oven rack and at least 2 inches away from the oven walls. (You may have to use two racks, depending on the size of your oven. If you do this, stagger the pans so that one doesn't bake directly on top of the other.) Bake until a cake tester inserted in the center comes out clean and dry, 27 to

32 minutes. Remove from the oven and let cool in the pans on wire racks for 10 minutes before turning them out onto the racks to cool completely before filling.

When ready to fill and finish the cake, place one layer, bottom side up, on a cake plate. Spread the lemon curd over the surface, leaving about ½ inch of the perimeter of the cake exposed (this is so the lemon curd won't leak down over the side of the cake when you position the top layer). Cut one-third of the strawberries into ¼-inch slices and use them to cover the lemon curd. Place the slices right up to the edge of the layer. Place the second layer, top side up, over the filling. Spread the whipped cream over the top of the cake (but not the sides). Arrange the whole strawberries on top.

This cake is best served within 2 hours after it has been assembled. It should remain refrigerated until serving.

NOTE: Prepared lemon curd is available in the baking section of most supermarkets and in specialty-food stores.

IN THE AUTUMN OF 1621, WHEN THE NEWLY ARRIVED PILGRIMS
SHARED THE BOUNTY OF THEIR HARVEST WITH KING MASSASOIT AND
NINETY OF HIS TRIBESMEN, THERE APPEARED ON THE
MENU MANY OF THE VERY SAME INGREDIENTS AND DISHES THAT
WE ENJOY TODAY. SWEET POTATOES WERE, I AM SAD TO SAY,
NOT AVAILABLE TO THOSE EARLY SETTLERS, BUT SINCE NO MODERN
THANKSGIVING FEAST WOULD BE THE SAME WITHOUT THEM,
I'VE NUDGED HISTORY JUST A BIT FOR THEIR SAKE.

cream of butternut squash soup

***

SERVES 10

With the color and consistency of gold velvet, this soup brings a glow to the table and makes a satisfying starter to any meal. Served hot with a hearty salad and loaf of bread, it's practically a meal in itself. Served cold, it will lower the temperature of the hottest summer day.

Heat the olive oil in a large soup pot over low heat. Add the onion and cook until soft, about 10 minutes. Add the squash, apples, thyme, sage, salt, pepper, and chicken broth. Bring to a boil, then lower the heat so that the mixture simmers. Simmer, uncovered, until the squash and apples are tender enough that a fork pierces the chunks with no resistance, about 45 minutes.

Use an immersion blender to purée the mixture, or carefully pour portions of the mixture into a food processor or blender and process or blend until the mixture is smooth. If you are using a food processor or blender to purée the soup, transfer each portion to a clean soup pot once it has been puréed. If you are using an immersion blender, the soup can remain in the pot. Add the cream or half-and-half and blend well. Reheat the soup without allowing it to boil. Ladle into warmed soup bowls. Sprinkle each serving with the minced sun-dried tomatoes and drizzle on about 1 teaspoon of the reserved sun-dried tomato oil.

The soup can be made up to 2 days ahead and stored in a covered container in the refrigerator. Reheat over low heat, stirring frequently, or serve cold, with the same garnish.

2 tablespoons mild olive oil

1 large onion, peeled and chopped

3 pounds peeled and seeded butternut squash flesh, cut into 2-inch chunks (from about 5 pounds whole squash, or use 3 pounds peeled and seeded butternut squash cubes available in the produce section of many supermarkets)

3 large, tart apples such as Granny Smith, peeled, cored, and roughly cut into eighths

1 tablespoon fresh thyme leaves or 1 teaspoon dried thyme

1 tablespoon fresh sage leaves or 1 teaspoon dried sage leaves

1 teaspoon salt

½ teaspoon freshly ground black pepper

10 cups (2½ quarts) canned low-sodium chicken broth, water, or a combination of broth and water

2 cups (16 ounces) light cream or half-and-half

¼ cup (1 ounce) oil-packed sun-dried tomatoes, drained (reserve the oil) and finely minced

roast turkey with giblet gravy

One 10- to 12-pound turkey

1 cup table salt or 2 cups
kosher salt

1 cup granulated sugar

2 tablespoons whole
black peppercorns

1 cinnamon stick

1 tablespoon whole cloves

1 tablespoon dried juniper berries

2 bay leaves

2 onions, peeled and
roughly chopped

4 carrots, peeled and
roughly chopped

4 stalks celery, roughly chopped

6 tablespoons (¾ stick; 3 ounces)
unsalted butter, at room temperature

¼ cup fresh sage leaves, slivered,
or 1 tablespoon dried sage

2 tablespoons fresh thyme leaves,
or 2 teaspoons dried thyme

1 tablespoon freshly ground
black pepper

2 tablespoons (1 ounce) unsalted
butter, melted

This recipe takes about 8 hours to make, which may seem like a daunting amount of time for the new or holiday-stressed cook. Keep in mind that for more than half of that time the turkey will be sitting in brine, leaving you to go about your business. The brining process—soaking meat or fowl in a mixture of water, salt, sugar, and spices—tenderizes and adds tremendous flavor. You can brine the turkey for as long as 24 hours or as little as 5 hours. If refrigerator space is an issue, you can put the brining bird in an unheated porch or garage— as long as the temperature remains below 40°F.

Remove the turkey giblets and neck and put them in a medium saucepan. Set aside until ready to make the gravy. Do not include the liver, as it will make the giblet stock bitter.

Rinse the turkey inside and out, pat it dry, and put it in a stockpot large enough to hold it comfortably. Add enough water to cover the turkey. Remove the turkey and set it aside. Add the salt, sugar, peppercorns, cinnamon stick, cloves, juniper berries, and bay leaves to the water in the pot. Bring to a boil, then reduce the heat and simmer for 10 minutes. Remove from the heat and let the brining liquid cool to room temperature, then put the turkey, breast side down, in the stockpot with the brining liquid. Cover the pot and put it in the refrigerator or other cold place (no warmer than 40°F) for at least 4 hours and up to 24 hours.

Three hours before you plan to serve the turkey, preheat the oven to 400°F. Oil a rack that will fit in a roasting pan large enough to hold the turkey and place the rack in the pan. In a medium bowl, mix together the roughly chopped onions, carrots, and celery. Scatter half of this mixture on the bottom of the roasting pan. Cover the vegetables with 2 cups of water. Remove the turkey from the brine and rinse it well under cool running water inside and out. Use paper towels to dry the turkey and place it on the oiled rack, breast side up. Place the remaining roughly chopped vegetables in the cavity of the turkey.

CONT'D

For the giblet stock and gravy:

1 onion, unpeeled, washed,
and quartered

2 carrots, peeled and cut crosswise
into 3 chunks each

2 stalks celery, cut crosswise into
4 chunks each

4 tablespoons (½ stick; 2 ounces)
unsalted butter

½ cup (2.5 ounces) unbleached
all-purpose flour

2 cups (16 ounces) canned
low-sodium chicken broth,
or as needed

Salt

Put 4 tablespoons of the room-temperature butter in a small mixing bowl and add the sage, thyme, and ground pepper and mix well. Gently slide your fingers between the skin and the breast meat of the turkey, loosening the membrane that connects them to create a pocket. Rub the herb butter as evenly as possible under the skin. Rub the skin all over with the remaining 2 tablespoons room-temperature butter.

Place the turkey in the oven and roast for 2 hours, basting every 30 minutes with the 2 tablespoons of melted butter and adding more water to the pan when the vegetables are dry. Check the temperature of the turkey; it is cooked through when an instant-read thermometer inserted into the thigh away from the bone registers 175°F. Transfer the turkey to a carving board and let rest for 20 minutes before carving.

As soon as the turkey goes into the oven, begin the gravy by making a giblet stock: Add the quartered onion, the 6 chunks of carrot, and the 8 chunks of celery to the giblets and neck in the saucepan. Add 4 cups of water and bring to a boil over medium-high heat. Turn the heat to low and allow the stock to simmer, uncovered, for 1½ hours. Remove the neck and giblets and set them aside. Strain the stock and allow it to cool; discard the vegetables that cooked in the stock. When the neck and giblets are cool enough to handle, remove the meat from the neck and finely chop the giblets, reserving the neck meat and giblets together in the refrigerator.

While the turkey is resting, complete the gravy: In a medium saucepan over medium-high heat, melt the 4 tablespoons butter. When the foam subsides, add the flour and stir for 2 minutes to brown the flour. Measure the reserved giblet stock and add enough chicken broth, if necessary, to make 3½ cups. Add the stock mixture to the flour mixture and whisk well. Bring to a simmer and cook, whisking often, until the gravy is thickened to the consistency of light cream, about 15 minutes. Season with salt to taste. Add the reserved chopped turkey neck meat and giblets, if desired, and serve the gravy with the turkey.

apple-chestnut corn bread stuffing

***

SERVES 10 TO 12

This recipe offers some shortcuts if you are pressed for time: use 3 or 4 large store-bought corn muffins crumbled into 1-inch bits, or substitute 16 ounces of packaged corn bread stuffing. And in lieu of roasting and peeling your own chestnuts (see page 50) you can purchase them in jars or vacuum-sealed plastic bags.

The corn bread can be made up to 3 days ahead. If using store-bought muffins or stuffing mix, add to the onion-apple sauté along with the chicken broth and chestnuts.

To make the corn bread, preheat the oven to 400°F with the rack in the center position. Generously butter an 8-inch square baking pan. In a medium mixing bowl, stir together the flour, cornmeal, baking powder, baking soda, and salt. Put the sour cream, eggs, and melted butter in a small mixing bowl and stir until smooth. Add the sour-cream mixture to the flour mixture and stir just to mix, until there is no more flour visible and no large lumps. Do not overmix, or the corn bread will be tough. Pour the batter into the prepared pan and bake for 20 to 25 minutes, or until a cake tester or toothpick comes out clean and the corn bread is golden brown and just begins to shrink from the sides of the pan. Remove from the oven and cool completely on a wire rack before unmolding.

Preheat the oven to 350°F with the rack in the center position. Break the corn bread into 1-inch pieces and scatter the pieces on a baking sheet or in a large roasting pan. Place in the oven for about 20 minutes, stirring once or twice, until toasted and dry. Let cool to warm before proceeding.

Melt the ½ cup butter in a large skillet over medium-high heat. Add the onion and celery and cook, stirring, until the vegetables are soft. Add the apples, sage, thyme, and salt and cook for another 3 minutes,

CONT'D

For the corn bread:

¾ cup (3.75 ounces) unbleached all-purpose flour

¾ cup (3.75 ounces) medium-grind yellow cornmeal

2 teaspoons baking powder

½ teaspoon baking soda

½ teaspoon salt

¾ cup (6 ounces) sour cream

2 extra-large eggs

4 tablespoons (½ stick; 2 ounces) unsalted butter, melted

½ cup (1 stick; 4 ounces) unsalted butter

1½ cups finely chopped onion

1 cup finely chopped celery

2 tart apples, peeled, cored, and chopped into ½-inch chunks

1½ teaspoons dried sage

1 teaspoon dried thyme

1 teaspoon salt

2 cups canned low-sodium chicken broth

20 chestnuts (7 ounces), chopped into ½-inch pieces (see page 50)

stirring occasionally, until the apples just begin to soften. Turn the vegetables into a large bowl and add the crumbled corn bread, the chicken broth, and the chestnuts. Stir gently to mix well.

Butter a 2½-quart baking dish and spoon the stuffing into the baking dish. Cover the dish with a piece of buttered or nonstick aluminum foil and bake for 25 to 30 minutes, until the stuffing is heated throughout. Uncover and bake about 15 minutes longer.

The unbaked stuffing can be made up to a day ahead and stored in the refrigerator, covered, in its baking dish; bake just before serving.

Preheat the oven to 300°F with the rack in the center position.

Lay a chestnut, flat side down, on a work surface. Use a small, very sharp knife to cut an X on the round side. Make sure to pierce the shell. Cut the remaining chestnuts in the same way. Place them, cut side up, in a large roasting pan, then add about ½ inch of hot water to the pan. Roast the chestnuts for 25 to 30 minutes, or until the cut sides begin to peel back and look dry.

Remove the pan from the oven and, as soon as the chestnuts are cool enough to handle (the hotter they are, the easier this job will be), peel off the shells. Ideally the brown skin under the shells will come off as well, but if it doesn't you can trim it away with a sharp knife. The peeled chestnuts are perishable even under refrigeration, so you should either prepare them no more than 2 days before you plan to use them, or prepare them several weeks in advance and freeze them in heavy-duty, zippered plastic bags.

anadama bread

MAKES 1 LOAF

10 ounces (1¼ cups) warm (skin temperature) water, plus additional if necessary

3 cups (15 ounces) unbleached all-purpose flour

1 tablespoon active dry yeast (not rapid rise)

1 tablespoon Lora Brody's Bread Dough Enhancer (optional, for a higher-rising loaf; see notes)

½ cup (2.5 ounces) medium-grind yellow cornmeal

2 scant teaspoons salt

3 tablespoons vegetable oil

3 tablespoons regular molasses (not blackstrap)

3 tablespoons hulled, unsalted sunflower seeds, toasted (see notes)

The story behind this bread with the strange name is that Anna's husband got tired of the cornmeal mush she fed him on a daily basis. Who knows if it was his muttering "Anna, damn her!" under his breath that got her to add flour, molasses, and yeast—or did he just make the bread himself, cursing her as he did so? Either way, and fact or fiction, that combination results in a hearty, rustic loaf that slices beautifully.

In the bowl of a stand mixer fitted with the dough hook, in a bread machine set on the dough cycle, or in a large mixing bowl, combine the water, flour, yeast, Dough Enhancer (if using), cornmeal, salt, oil, and molasses. Knead or mix until a sticky dough forms, then continue kneading for about 8 minutes until a smooth, slightly sticky ball forms. Place the dough in a large, lightly greased bowl, cover with plastic wrap, and let rise in a warm place until it has increased in bulk by one-third and looks slightly puffy.

Coat the sides and bottom of an 8-cup loaf pan with a little vegetable oil. Gently deflate the dough and knead in the sunflower seeds. Place the dough in the prepared pan, cover with plastic wrap, and let rise in a warm place until it has almost doubled in bulk.

Preheat the oven to 375°F with the rack in the center position. Bake the bread for 35 to 40 minutes, or until the interior registers 200°F on an instant-read thermometer and the loaf is crusty, deep brown, and feels firm when tapped on top. Remove the bread from the pan and let cool on a wire rack before slicing.

NOTES: Lora Brody's Bread Dough Enhancer is available at www.lorabrody.com, 888-9-Bakeit, or at the King Arthur Flour Baker's Catalogue, www.kingarthurflour.com, 800-827-6836.

To toast sunflower seeds, preheat the oven to 350°F with the rack in the center position. Place the raw seeds on a heavy-duty, rimmed baking sheet in a single layer and bake, stirring occasionally, until they are golden brown and fragrant, about 15 minutes.

mashed sweet potatoes

4 to 5 large sweet potatoes (about 4½ pounds), scrubbed

¾ cup (1½ sticks; 6 ounces) unsalted butter, at room temperature

2 teaspoons ground cinnamon

1 teaspoon ground nutmeg

¾ cup (6 ounces) firmly packed dark brown sugar

3 extra-large eggs

¾ cup (6 ounces) whole milk

What would Thanksgiving be without sweet potatoes?
Even though they weren't on the Pilgrims' menu,
most of us can't imagine the turkey without them.
This dish can be assembled up to a day in advance and baked
just before serving, and it can be baked anywhere in the oven
(which makes room for all the other things
that need to be accommodated).

Preheat the oven to 375°F with the rack in the center position. Butter a baking dish with sides at least 2 inches deep and a 10-cup capacity; set aside.

Bake the sweet potatoes in their skins for 1 hour, until tender enough that a fork pierces them with no resistance. Reduce the oven temperature to 350°F. Remove the potatoes from their skins and put them in a large bowl. Add the butter, cinnamon, nutmeg, and brown sugar and mix well. Mix the eggs with the milk and add to the potatoes in the bowl. Mix well and pour the mixture into the prepared baking dish. Bake until hot throughout, 20 to 30 minutes.

cranberry and pear chutney

***

**I consider chutney an underutilized condiment.
Just think of all the things you can serve it with to make a regular
meal into something really special: roast turkey, beef,
and lamb all benefit from the glamour and pizzazz chutney
delivers to the plate as well as to the palate.**

**My favorite application is to use it in place of
mustard or mayo on a sandwich, particularly
the turkey and cheddar one on page 175.
When you see how easy it is to make your own chutney,
perhaps you'll think of it next time you need
a holiday or hostess gift, as it keeps, refrigerated in
tightly covered containers, for several months.
It is best served at room temperature.**

2 cups (7 ounces) fresh or frozen cranberries

4 large, slightly underripe Comice pears, peeled, cored, and cut into ½-inch dice

½ cup (2 ounces) golden raisins

1 large sweet onion such as Vidalia, peeled and diced

⅔ cup (5.4 ounces) orange juice

½ cup (4 ounces) pure maple syrup

¼ cup (2 ounces) regular molasses (not blackstrap)

1½ tablespoons peeled and grated fresh gingerroot

Finely grated zest and juice of 2 limes (about 1 heaping tablespoon of zest and 1 tablespoon plus one teaspoon of juice)

2 teaspoons salt

1 teaspoon freshly ground black pepper

1 teaspoon ground cardamom

½ teaspoon ground nutmeg

½ teaspoon ground allspice

Combine the cranberries, pears, raisins, onion, orange juice, maple syrup, molasses, gingerroot, lime zest and juice, salt, pepper, cardamom, nutmeg, and allspice in a large saucepan and place over medium-high heat. Stir to combine with a wooden spoon and bring the mixture to a simmer. Reduce the heat and cook, uncovered, over medium-low heat for 1 hour, stirring occasionally, until the pears have softened and the liquid has reduced slightly. Remove from the heat. Let cool for 20 minutes at room temperature, then transfer to a covered container and let cool completely in the refrigerator. (The chutney will thicken as it cools.) Bring to room temperature before serving.

indian pudding

½ cup (2.5 ounces) medium-grind yellow cornmeal

4 cups (32 ounces) whole milk

¼ cup (2 ounces) regular molasses (not blackstrap)

1 extra-large egg, lightly beaten

2 tablespoons (1 ounce) unsalted butter, cut into 4 pieces

2 tablespoons granulated sugar

1 teaspoon ground ginger

½ teaspoon ground cinnamon

¼ teaspoon salt

⅛ teaspoon grated nutmeg

⅛ teaspoon ground cloves

⅛ teaspoon baking soda

Vanilla ice cream for serving (optional)

For someone who is licking his or her lips in anticipation of a more traditional dessert like pumpkin pie, Indian pudding may at first glance be a disappointment. It has none of the glamour of pie or the predictable flavor of cake, but it's got so many other great attributes, in many ways it's better than pie and cake. It may not be the most beautiful end to a meal, but the combination of its hot puddinglike interior, its slightly crusty top cradled by a small lake of melting vanilla ice cream, and the dreamy aromas of spices and molasses put Indian pudding in a dessert class all its own.

Preheat the oven to 300°F with the rack in the center position. Lightly butter a 2-quart, round, straight-sided baking dish such as an 8-inch soufflé dish; set aside.

Place the cornmeal in a large, heavy-bottomed saucepan. Slowly whisk in 2 cups of the milk. When the mixture is smooth, with no lumps, whisk in the remaining 2 cups of milk, the molasses, egg, and butter. In a small bowl, combine the sugar with the ginger, cinnamon, salt, nutmeg, cloves, and baking soda; stir the spice mixture into the cornmeal mixture.

Place the saucepan over medium-high heat. Stirring constantly, bring the mixture to a simmer. Continue to stir carefully, reaching into the corners of the saucepan, and bring the mixture to a boil. Boil gently for 30 seconds, stirring constantly, then remove from the heat. Pour the mixture into the prepared baking dish. Bake until the pudding bubbles around the edges and the surface darkens slightly, about 1½ hours.

Let cool on a wire rack for 15 to 20 minutes, then serve warm, with a scoop of vanilla ice cream, if desired.

This pudding is best when eaten warm. To reheat the cooked and cooled pudding, cover the baking dish with aluminum foil and place it in a wider skillet of simmering water. Heat the baking dish in the simmering water for 15 to 20 minutes, or until the pudding is hot.

ON HALLOWEEN NIGHT IN THE CITY OF
SALEM, MASSACHUSETTS, ANY WITCH YOU MIGHT SEE
WILL HAVE TRICK OR TREAT ON HIS OR HER MIND. GOBLINS
AND GHOSTS WILL BE OUT IN FORCE AS WELL,
SO PLAN AHEAD, AND NO MATTER WHERE YOU CELEBRATE
ALL HALLOWS' EVE, THE PRANKSTERS ON YOUR BLOCK
WILL COME BACK FOR SECONDS.

sparklers (sweet and spicy roasted pumpkin seeds)

vegetable chili in a pumpkin tureen

caramel apples

dirt cake

halloween cupcakes

sparklers
(sweet and spicy roasted pumpkin seeds)

***

MAKES ABOUT 2 CUPS

These are better than roasted peanuts!

Preheat the oven to 250°F with the rack in the center position. Line a baking sheet with aluminum foil or a silicone pan liner. Put the pumpkin seeds in a bowl and drizzle the olive oil over them. Sprinkle the seeds with the salt, Worcestershire sauce, brown sugar, and Tabasco to taste, then toss the seeds well. Spread the seeds on the prepared baking sheet and bake for 1½ hours, or until the seeds are golden brown. Let cool completely on the baking sheet.

Store the toasted seeds in an airtight container at room temperature for up to 3 days.

2 cups raw pumpkin seeds, rinsed of pumpkin fibers and dried well on paper towels

2 tablespoons olive oil

1 teaspoon kosher salt

1 tablespoon Worcestershire sauce

1 tablespoon dark brown sugar

A few drops of Tabasco or other hot-pepper sauce

vegetable chili in a pumpkin tureen

* * *

SERVES 10

2 tablespoons olive oil

2 onions, peeled and roughly chopped into ½-inch dice

4 large carrots, peeled and sliced into ½-inch rounds

4 celery stalks, cut into ½-inch slices

3 medium leeks, white parts only, washed well and cut into ¼-inch rounds

1 bulb fennel, trimmed, cored, and cut into ½-inch dice

5 cloves garlic, peeled and minced

1½ teaspoons whole cumin seeds

1 teaspoon dried oregano

2 tablespoons mild chili powder

2 teaspoons salt

2 large sweet potatoes, peeled and cut into 1-inch pieces

3 large yellow potatoes, peeled and cut into 1-inch pieces

One 20-ounce can chickpeas, drained and rinsed

One 15-ounce can pinto beans, drained and rinsed

Two 28-ounce cans crushed tomatoes

8 ounces mushrooms, brushed clean and sliced

1 cup fresh or frozen corn kernels

1½ cups frozen peas

¼ cup fresh flat-leaf (Italian) parsley, finely chopped

1 large (6 to 8 pounds) sugar pumpkin

I thought it might be nice for the adults to have something to eat while the kids are gorging themselves with sweets, and then realized that the novelty of a stew served in a pumpkin might make even the most ardent vegetable-avoiding child at least try a bite. The chili, which is ideally made in a 6-quart slow cooker but can also be made in a Dutch oven, will keep in the refrigerator for up to 3 days before serving.

Don't be intimidated by the long list of ingredients; the stew goes together very quickly and needs little or no attention during the cooking time—especially if you use a slow cooker.

Make sure you note the interior measurements of your oven when you go shopping for a pumpkin.

To make the chili in a slow cooker: Heat the olive oil in a large skillet over medium-high heat. Add the onions, carrots, and celery and cook, stirring occasionally, for about 3 minutes, until the vegetables begin to soften. Add the leeks and fennel and cook for 2 minutes more. Add the garlic and cook for 1 minute, until it is fragrant. Make a space in the center of the skillet and add the cumin seeds. Allow them to toast for 1 minute, then stir them into the vegetables, along with the oregano, chili powder, and salt. Pour the vegetable mixture into the slow cooker pot and add the sweet potatoes, yellow potatoes, chickpeas, pinto beans, tomatoes, and 1 cup water, stirring well to combine. Cover and cook in the slow cooker for about 3 hours on high setting or about 5 hours on low setting, or until the potatoes are just tender. Add the mushrooms and cook for 1 hour more. Ten minutes before serving, add the corn, peas, and parsley and cook for 10 minutes more.

To make the chili in a Dutch oven: In a large Dutch oven or heavy soup kettle, heat the olive oil over medium-high heat. Add the onions, carrots, and celery and cook, stirring occasionally, for about 3 minutes, until the vegetables begin to soften. Add the leeks and fennel and cook for 2 minutes more. Add the garlic and cook for 1 minute, until it is fragrant. Make a space in the center of the pot and add the cumin seeds. Allow them to toast for 1 minute, then stir them into the vegetables, along with the oregano, chili powder, and salt. Add the sweet potatoes, yellow potatoes, chickpeas, pinto beans, tomatoes, and 2 cups water, stirring well to combine. Bring just to a boil and cover. Reduce the heat to low and simmer for about 2 hours, or until the potatoes are just tender. Add the mushrooms and cook for 30 minutes more. Ten minutes before serving, add the corn, peas, and parsley and cook for 10 minutes more.

About an hour before serving, preheat the oven to 350°F with the rack in the lowest position. Use a sharp, serrated knife to slice off the top of the pumpkin as you would for a jack-o'-lantern, and reserve it. Use a long-handled metal spoon to scrape and scoop out the seeds and as much of the stringy fibers as possible. Reserve the seeds to roast (see page 59). Place the pumpkin in a large, lightly oiled roasting pan, then apply a light coating of vegetable oil to the surface of the pumpkin. Oil the top and place it next to the pumpkin in the roasting pan. The cooking time will vary with the weight of the pumpkin, but figure on at least 40 minutes. You want the outside of the pumpkin soft enough to be easily pierced with the tip of a sharp knife, yet not so soft that it collapses.

Remove the pumpkin from the oven, carefully transfer it to a large platter (the easiest way is to lift it with your hands, wearing oven mitts), ladle in the hot stew, then place the lid on top for presentation. Serve immediately by removing the lid and spooning out the stew; be sure to scrape portions of the cooked pumpkin flesh into each serving.

caramel apples

12 medium, crisp apples, thoroughly washed and dried, at room temperature

2 cups (16 ounces) firmly packed brown sugar

1 cup (2 sticks; 8 ounces) unsalted butter

14 ounces sweetened condensed milk

½ cup (4 ounces) pure maple syrup

⅓ cup (3 ounces) dark corn syrup

⅓ cup (3 ounces) light corn syrup

1 tablespoon regular molasses (not blackstrap)

2 teaspoons pure vanilla extract

½ teaspoon salt

½ teaspoon fresh lemon juice

Kids love these and grown-ups wince at the sight of them, knowing that decaramelizing the kids will be a follow-up challenge. The best apples to use here are crisp, fairly tart varieties like Jonathan, Braeburn, Ida Red, or McIntosh. Most apples come coated with a waxy substance to keep them fresh, which makes it hard for the caramel to adhere, so wash them in warm water and dry them well before you start. Also, making sure they are at room temperature will prevent the caramel from setting before the entire apple has been coated.

Poke skewers or chopsticks almost all the way through each apple from the stem end (top) to the blossom end (bottom), but do not allow the skewers or chopsticks to protrude all the way through the bottom of the apples.

In a medium saucepan over medium-high heat, combine the brown sugar, butter, sweetened condensed milk, maple syrup, dark and light corn syrups, molasses, vanilla, salt, and lemon juice. Cook, stirring constantly, until the butter is melted and the mixture comes to a boil. Occasionally wet a pastry brush with cold water and brush around the sides of the pan. Insert a candy thermometer (one that will measure temperatures to at least 250°F in one- or two-degree increments) into the pot and continue to heat, stirring, until the temperature reaches 238°F, about 15 minutes. Immediately remove the caramel from the heat and let cool to 210°F.

One by one, dip the apples into the caramel, using the skewer or chopstick as a handle. Coat the apples completely. Place the coated apples, stem side up (so that the skewers or chopsticks are sticking up), on a piece of buttered aluminum foil or parchment paper and let cool in the refrigerator.

Apples can be made up to a day ahead.

dirt cake

One 18-ounce package chocolate sandwich cookies

4 tablespoons (½ stick; 2 ounces) unsalted butter, at room temperature

8 ounces cream cheese, at room temperature

½ cup (2 ounces) confectioners' sugar

½ teaspoon pure vanilla extract

2 cups (16 ounces) skim milk

1 cup (8 ounces) half-and-half

Two 3-ounce packages instant chocolate pudding mix

One 12-ounce container frozen whipped topping mix, thawed

3 ounces gummy worms

Here's a project for parents and kids to do together. There's no baking involved. Be as creative as you wish; you can make the cake in a plastic pumpkin (the size that children use for trick or treating), or even a hollowed-out real one that is no more than about 10 inches in diameter, although the real pumpkin is much more work since it must be scraped out well before using. Both the plastic and the real pumpkin should be lined with aluminum foil before adding the pudding. For a spookier version, use one of the "life-size" hollow plastic skulls that are sold in stores around Halloween time. The cake can also be made in an ungreased, unlined 9-by-13-inch baking pan.

In a food processor, process the cookies to fine crumbs. (This can also be done by placing the cookies in a heavy-duty zippered plastic bag and crushing them with a rolling pin.) You should have 4 cups of crumbs. Set the crumbs aside.

Put the butter, cream cheese, confectioners' sugar, and vanilla in a large bowl or the bowl of a stand mixer and beat until smooth. Add the milk, half-and-half, and chocolate pudding mix to the bowl and continue to beat until smooth. Add the whipped topping mix and beat on low speed until no white streaks remain.

Spoon about half of the chocolate mixture into a hollow plastic or real pumpkin that has been lined with aluminum foil, or into an ungreased 9-by-13-inch pan. Pour about half of the cookie crumbs over the chocolate mixture, then spoon the remaining chocolate mixture on top of the crumbs. Sprinkle the remaining crumbs over the top. Lay the gummy worms over the top layer of crumbs, poking some of them through the crumbs into the pudding mixture so that only parts of the worms are visible. Chill in the refrigerator for at least 3 hours and up to 8 hours before serving.

halloween cupcakes

For the filling:

8 ounces cream cheese, at
room temperature

⅓ cup (3 ounces) granulated sugar

1 extra-large egg

Pinch of salt

17 drops yellow food coloring and
7 drops red food coloring

For the cupcakes:

2 cups (10 ounces) unbleached
all-purpose flour

½ cup (1.6 ounces) unsweetened
natural (not Dutch-processed)
cocoa powder, sifted

1 teaspoon baking powder

½ teaspoon baking soda

½ teaspoon salt

¾ cup (1½ sticks; 6 ounces)
unsalted butter, at room
temperature

2 cups (16 ounces)
granulated sugar

3 extra-large eggs

½ cup (4 ounces) sour cream

¾ cup (6 ounces) whole milk

**Let the kids lend a hand when you make these special
Halloween treats; there's a good chance you'll inspire them to
keep on baking. The base is a simple but wonderfully
moist and flavorful chocolate cupcake into which a filling
of orange-colored cream cheese is dropped just before baking.
As the cupcakes rise, the filling becomes a topping
that swirls around the tops, creating a marblelike design.**

Preheat the oven to 350°F with the rack in the center position. Coat the
cups of two 12-cup muffin tins with butter, or lightly butter only the
flat top of the tin and line the cups with paper or foil liners. Set aside.

To make the filling, place the cream cheese, sugar, egg, and salt in
the bowl of a food processor and process until the mixture is smooth.
Add the food coloring and mix until the color is uniform. Set aside.

To make the cupcakes, sift the flour, cocoa powder, baking powder,
baking soda, and salt into a medium bowl. Set aside. Place the butter
and sugar in a large mixing bowl. With an electric mixer on medium
speed, beat the butter and sugar until light and fluffy. With the mixer
still on medium speed, add the eggs, one at a time, mixing well after
each addition. Beat in the sour cream, scraping down the sides of the
bowl with a rubber spatula as you work. Reduce the mixer speed to
low and add about one-third of the flour mixture. Mix well, then add
about half the milk, and mix well. Continue adding the flour and milk,
mixing well after each addition, ending with flour.

Use a ¼-cup measure to fill each prepared muffin cup three-fourths full of batter. Drop about 1 tablespoon of the cream cheese filling on top of each cup of batter. Bake the cupcakes until they have risen somewhat, the tops spring back when lightly pressed, and a cake tester inserted in a cake center comes out clean, 20 to 22 minutes. Let the cupcakes cool in the pan for 10 minutes, then transfer them to a wire rack to cool completely.

The cooled cupcakes can be stored in an airtight container in the refrigerator for up to 3 days.

Connecticut

The **Nutmeg State** has it all, from rolling hills to sandy beaches. You can view world-class art, wander through stunning gardens, and go white-water kayaking. Take a hike on the **Appalachian Trail** or stroll through autumn leaf–strewn college campuses. Stay in a charming bed-and-breakfast, put together a picnic from a farm stand, and bike over winding backcountry roads. Take your time to explore its many charms—**Connecticut** will delight you.

THERE IS NOTHING LIKE SUN AND SALT AIR
TO CREATE HEARTY APPETITES. LISTEN FOR
THE SNAP OF ROPES AGAINST MASTS,
THE FLUTTER OF FLAGS FLYING, AND THE CRY OF GULLS
WHO WOULD BE MORE THAN HAPPY
TO SHARE A FEW BITES OF
YOUR WELCOME-TO-SUMMER BREAKFAST.

raspberry champagne coolers

page NO. 71

asparagus salad with lemon vinaigrette

page NO. 72

streusel-topped stuffed french toast

page NO. 74

breakfast sausage

page NO. 76

raspberry champagne coolers

***

SERVES 6

If you've done the mimosa thing and are looking for something a bit new and different, then consider the following libation, which makes an absolutely delightful beginning to any festive occasion. The recipe calls for frozen raspberries because they are juicier once they thaw and it is easier to strain them.

For the Seedless Raspberry Purée:

One 10-ounce package frozen raspberries

2 tablespoons granulated sugar, or more to taste

1 teaspoon fresh lemon juice

Two 750-ml bottles Champagne, Prosecco, or other sparkling white wine, well chilled

½ pint (1 cup) fresh raspberries

To make the raspberry purée, thaw the raspberries in their package in the refrigerator. Pour them into a fine-mesh strainer set over a bowl and press on them with the back of a spoon until all that is left in the strainer are the seeds. Add the sugar and lemon juice to the puréed berries and stir. Taste and add more sugar if desired.

For each drink, place 1 tablespoon of raspberry purée in a Champagne flute. When guests arrive, pour the Champagne or sparkling wine over the purée. Float a few fresh raspberries in each glass.

asparagus salad with lemon vinaigrette

* * *

SERVES 6 TO 8

1 tablespoon salt

3 pounds asparagus, woody ends trimmed

For the vinaigrette:

Finely grated zest of 1 lemon

3 tablespoons fresh lemon juice, strained

1 teaspoon Dijon mustard

½ teaspoon granulated sugar

½ teaspoon kosher or coarse salt

¼ teaspoon freshly ground black pepper

⅔ cup mild olive oil

1 tablespoon chopped fresh chives

Salad for breakfast may be a bit unusual, but this festive preparation offers a nice alternative to fruit. While fresh asparagus is now available year round, thanks to air express, the very best shows up in the markets and on farmstands in early spring. For this salad, either the pencil-thin stalks or the thicker kind are fine—just make sure to adjust the cooking time so that the thin spears are not overcooked and the fat ones are just tender. If you are using the thick stalks, use a vegetable peeler to remove the tough outer skin just below the tips.

Fill a wide 6- to 8-quart saucepan about one-third full of water. Add the salt and bring to a boil. Add the asparagus, return to a boil, then reduce the heat to low and simmer the asparagus just until tender, 3 to 4 minutes for thin stalks and up to 7 minutes for thick stalks. Drain the asparagus well in a colander.

To make the vinaigrette, in a medium bowl, whisk together the lemon zest and juice, mustard, sugar, salt, and pepper. Add the olive oil in a very thin, steady stream, whisking vigorously as the oil is added. Continue to whisk until all the oil is added and the mixture has thickened a bit.

Just before serving, arrange the asparagus on a serving platter and drizzle the vinaigrette over. Sprinkle the chopped chives over the asparagus and vinaigrette.

The asparagus can be cooked up to a day ahead and refrigerated. The vinaigrette can be made up to 3 days ahead and refrigerated separately. Bring both to room temperature before serving.

streusel-topped stuffed french toast

***

For the streusel topping:

⅔ cup (2.5 ounces) pecans, toasted (see note) and coarsely chopped

⅓ cup (2.5 ounces) firmly packed dark brown sugar

⅓ cup (1.5 ounces) unbleached all-purpose flour

1 teaspoon ground cinnamon

¼ teaspoon salt

½ teaspoon freshly grated orange zest

3 tablespoons (1½ ounces) unsalted butter, at room temperature, cut into pieces

For the French toast:

6 ounces regular cream cheese (not whipped or reduced fat), at room temperature

Scant ½ cup (4 ounces) raspberry preserves, or other preserves of your choice

1 loaf challah or other rich egg bread, ends trimmed, cut into six 1½-inch-thick slices

1 cup (8 ounces) whole milk

4 extra-large eggs

⅓ cup (2.5 ounces) firmly packed dark brown sugar

½ teaspoon ground cinnamon

¼ teaspoon pure vanilla extract

Attention big breakfast lovers! You have come to the right place. These scrumptious, warm pockets filled with raspberry cream and coated with a crunchy toasted topping before they are baked in the oven will satisfy any and all empty bellies looking for a satisfying (and filling) beginning to the day.

I suggest assembling these the day before just to the point where they are to go in the oven. Refrigerate them in their baking dish, then bake just before serving.

Preheat the oven to 350°F with the rack in the center position. Line a rimmed baking sheet with parchment paper or a silicone pan liner. If using parchment, spray lightly with nonstick vegetable spray.

To make the streusel topping, combine the pecans, brown sugar, flour, cinnamon, salt, and orange zest in a medium bowl and mix well with a fork. Add the butter pieces and, using your fingertips, work to distribute the butter evenly throughout the topping until large clumps form. Set aside.

To make the French toast, whisk together the cream cheese and preserves in a small bowl until the mixture is uniform and fairly smooth. (It's okay if some small bits of cream cheese remain visible.) Set aside.

Using a small, sharp knife, cut a 2-inch slit in the bottom crust of each bread slice, and continue cutting into the bread to make a pocket in the slice. (Be careful not to make the initial cut any wider than 2 inches and don't cut through any of the remaining three sides with your knife, or the topping will seep out during baking.) Use a very small spoon (a baby spoon is perfect, if you happen to have one) to fill each of the pockets with an equal portion of the cream cheese and preserves mixture.

In a medium mixing bowl, whisk together the milk, eggs, brown sugar, cinnamon, and vanilla. Pour into a flat, rimmed dish.

Working with 2 pieces of stuffed bread at a time, use a wide metal spatula to slide the pieces into the batter. Let the first side soak for 2 minutes. Use the spatula to turn the bread over and soak the second side for 2 minutes. Place the soaked breads on the prepared baking sheet. Continue with the remaining stuffed bread slices and lay them side by side on the pan.

Sprinkle the streusel topping evenly over the tops of the soaked bread slices. (At this point the French toast can be covered and refrigerated overnight, or it can be frozen in a tightly sealed, flat plastic container. Allow the container to thaw overnight in the refrigerator before transferring to a prepared baking sheet and following the baking instructions below.)

Bake for 35 minutes, or until the tops and sides of the bread are golden brown, the topping is crisp, and the surface springs back lightly when pressed lightly with your finger. If bread feels soft or wet, continue baking for a few more minutes. Serve hot, either whole pieces for large servings or cut in half for smaller portions.

NOTE: To toast pecans, preheat the oven to 350°F with the rack in the center position. Place the nuts on a heavy-duty, rimmed baking sheet in a single layer and bake, stirring occasionally, until they are golden brown and fragrant, 10 to 12 minutes.

breakfast sausage

***

Breakfast sausages are short, narrow links
that cook up in no time and come in a dazzling choice of flavors
from traditional pork to turkey or chicken with all sorts
of added fruits, herbs, and spices, and can even be vegetarian.
Count on 3 to 4 links per person (don't forget they will be smaller
after they are cooked). You can broil them in the oven or
sauté them over medium-high heat. Either way,
cook the sausages until they are browned and quite crisp.
It may be necessary to drain off any collected fat partway through
the cooking time to ensure the sausages aren't greasy.
Drain them on a baking sheet lined with several layers
of paper towels just before serving.

SOME SAY THE HARVARD-YALE RIVALRY IS
AS ANCIENT AS THE INSTITUTIONS THEMSELVES.
I SAY, AS LONG AS THE FOOD IS
PLENTIFUL AND GOOD AND THE WEATHER
COOPERATES, I DON'T CARE WHO WINS.

celebration punch
page N°. 78

grilled chicken sandwiches with russian dressing
page N°. 79

crimson slaw
page N°. 80

nutmeg cookies
page N°. 81

celebration punch

* * *

SERVES ABOUT 25

2 whole seedless oranges,
peeled and cut into 1-inch chunks,
or two 12-ounce cans mandarin
oranges, drained

One 16-ounce can pineapple
chunks, drained

One 12-ounce can frozen lemonade
concentrate, thawed

One 12-ounce can frozen orange
juice concentrate, thawed

One 12-ounce can frozen limeade
concentrate, thawed

1½ quarts (48 ounces)
pineapple juice

2 cups (16 ounces) cranberry juice

1 quart (32 ounces) water

1 liter club soda

2 liters ginger ale

**A punch bowl chilled by a floating ring of citrus-studded
ice is hardly a new concept—in fact, it's such a far throwback that
I'm betting there's a whole new generation who has
never even heard of the idea. For those of you who do remember
those elegant punch bowls with floating, frozen islands,
this recipe will hopefully bring back memories of
other happy events of the past.**

Place the orange and pineapple chunks in a Bundt or other decorative
baking pan, fill the pan to within 1 inch of the rim with water, and
place the pan in the freezer. Freeze the ice ring until solid, at least
8 hours.

In a large bowl, mix together the thawed lemonade, orange juice, and
limeade concentrates. Add the pineapple juice, cranberry juice, and
water. Mix well. Refrigerate, covered, until you are ready to serve
the punch.

To serve, pour the chilled juice mixture into a punch bowl or other
suitable serving bowl large enough to hold the completed punch plus
the ice ring. Remove the ice ring container from the freezer and invert
it onto a large plate. Place a dish towel that has been soaked in hot
water over the bottom of the container to help release the ice ring.
Float the fruited ice ring in the juice mixture. Add the club soda and
ginger ale, and serve.

grilled chicken sandwiches with russian dressing

***

SERVES 8

Yum. That says it all. These juicy sandwiches had us all leaning over our plates so the drips wouldn't land in our laps. There were no complaints from the assembled fans, who I know for sure were already thinking about seconds as they wolfed down their firsts. The real keys to success here are marinating the chicken for at least the suggested 4 hours (although overnight is even better), and making sure not to overcook the chicken, which will make it tough. Serving these hot off the grill will warm the insides of all your football fans and make you the most popular player of the day.

To make the marinade, whisk together the oil, garlic, tomato paste, vinegar, soy sauce, and molasses in a small bowl. Pour into a heavy-duty, zippered plastic bag.

Place the chicken breasts between two pieces of wax paper and pound thin by smacking them several times with a small, heavy skillet. Put the chicken breasts in the bag with the marinade and refrigerate for at least 4 hours and up to overnight.

To make the Russian dressing, whisk together the mayonnaise, ketchup, relish, soy sauce, and Tabasco to taste in a medium bowl until well combined. The dressing can be made up to 4 days ahead. Refrigerate, covered, until ready to serve.

Prepare a fire in a charcoal grill or preheat a gas grill. Remove the chicken from the marinade and grill, brushing once or twice with the marinade, for about 3 minutes on each side, or until opaque throughout.

To serve, place an open onion roll on each of 8 plates and slather both cut surfaces with Russian dressing. Place a grilled chicken breast on one half and top with slices of red onion and avocado.

For the marinade:

½ cup (4 ounces) vegetable oil

2 cloves garlic, smashed

2 tablespoons tomato paste

¼ cup (2 ounces) red wine vinegar

¼ cup (2 ounces) soy sauce

1 tablespoon regular molasses (not blackstrap)

4 whole skinless, boneless chicken breasts, halved

For the Russian dressing:

⅔ cup (5 ounces) good-quality mayonnaise

⅓ cup (3 ounces) ketchup

¼ cup (2 ounces) sweet pickle relish

1 tablespoon soy sauce

A few drops of Tabasco or other hot-pepper sauce

8 onion rolls, halved

1 large red onion, peeled and sliced into rings

2 avocados, halved, pitted, and peeled, each half cut into 4 slices to make 16 slices

crimson slaw

4 large fresh beets (about 2½ pounds), washed and trimmed, or an equal amount of canned whole beets, well drained

1 cup (8 ounces) heavy cream

¼ cup (2 ounces) raspberry vinegar

2 tablespoons dark brown sugar

1 teaspoon caraway seeds

No matter which fight song you are singing, you'll find this tangy salad easier to swallow than the defeat of your favorite team. If you're in a big hurry to secure your spot at the stadium parking lot, you can certainly use canned beets in this recipe.

Be forewarned that everything in your general vicinity will turn pink as you work with the beets. You would be well advised to wear an apron and move your grandmother's hand-crocheted linen napkins well across the room, and perhaps don thin latex gloves to keep your hands unstained.

If you are using fresh beets, prepare an ice bath by filling a large bowl with several handfuls of ice cubes and covering them with cold water. Set aside. Bring a large pot of salted water to a rolling boil. Drop in the fresh beets and cook for about 8 minutes, or until the beets are tender enough to be easily pierced with the tip of a sharp knife. Use a slotted spoon to transfer the beets to the ice bath. When cool enough to handle, use a vegetable peeler or a small paring knife to remove the skins. Shred the beets, cooked or canned, using either a food processor fitted with the medium shredding blade or the large holes of a handheld grater.

Put the heavy cream in a 6-cup saucepan (the size will help prevent the cream from boiling over) and bring to a simmer over medium-high heat. Continue to cook the cream until it is reduced to ½ cup, 10 to 15 minutes. (You may need to move the pot on and off the heat a few times if the cream threatens to boil over.) Strain the cream into a small bowl and let cool slightly, 2 or 3 minutes. Whisk in the raspberry vinegar and brown sugar and combine well.

To assemble the salad, place the beets in a serving bowl and drizzle with the dressing. Toss well to coat all of the beets evenly and sprinkle them with caraway seeds. Serve cold or at room temperature.

The slaw can be made up to 3 days ahead and stored in a covered container in the refrigerator.

nutmeg cookies

***

There are many theories about why Connecticut is called
the Nutmeg State. My two favorites were supplied
by Judith Ellen Johnson, a genealogist at the Connecticut
Historical Society in Hartford. The first, according to
one Bruce Daniels in a Connecticut Historical Bulletin article
entitled "Nicknames of Connecticut," is that
"The name, first used in the generation after the Revolution,
derives from the alleged peddling of wooden nutmegs
in the Southern states by itinerant and unscrupulous
Connecticut tinsmiths." ("There is," Ms. Johnson said,
"among our museum objects, a curious device that unfortunately
lends credence to this theory.") "The nicer explanation,"
she continued, "comes from a series of radio blurbs that
our staff put together quite a number of years ago and
is equally plausible: Nutmegs grow on trees in the tropics, so how
did Connecticut, thousands of miles away, come to be known
as the Nutmeg State? Apparently the link was forged by the
Connecticut peddlers who bought goods imported and
manufactured by the state and sold them to Southern buyers.
Among his goods, the Yankee peddler carried nutmegs,
imported by Connecticut from the tropics.
The Southerners who purchased the nutmegs were puzzled
about how to use them, and tried to crack them with
a hammer, not realizing that the nutmegs had to be grated to
get the pungent powder used to season cakes and pies.
The hammer only made the nutmegs bounce, so the buyers
concluded that they were made of wood. This misunderstanding
led them to view the Yankee peddler as a shrewd trickster
and to call Connecticut 'the wooden nutmeg.'"

Whichever explanation you believe (or even if you have one of
your own), there is no better showcase for this hard-to-crack
"nut" (actually the seed of a tropical evergreen tree) than these
spice-filled cookies that will fill your kitchen with the aroma
and promise of something very good to eat.

2¼ cups (12.5 ounces) unbleached all-purpose flour

2 teaspoons baking soda

¼ teaspoon salt

1 teaspoon ground cinnamon

2 teaspoons ground nutmeg

¼ teaspoon ground cloves

¾ cup (1½ sticks; 6 ounces) unsalted butter

1 cup (8 ounces) firmly packed dark brown sugar

1 extra-large egg

¼ cup (2 ounces) regular molasses (not blackstrap)

⅓ cup (2.67 ounces) granulated sugar

CONT'D

NUTMEG COOKIES WITH HOT SPICED MAPLE—GRAND MARNIER TEA

see page Nᵒ. 165 *for the tea*

Preheat the oven to 375°F with 2 racks placed as close to the center of the oven as possible. Line 2 baking sheets with aluminum foil or silicone pan liners. If you are using foil, butter it or spray it with nonstick vegetable spray.

In a medium bowl, whisk together the flour, baking soda, salt, cinnamon, 1 teaspoon of the nutmeg, and cloves. Set aside. With an electric mixer on high speed, beat the butter and brown sugar until light and fluffy, about 2 minutes. Add the egg and molasses and beat for about 1 minute, until the mixture comes together and no longer looks curdled. Scrape the sides of the bowl as you work. Add the flour mixture and mix on low speed just until it is all incorporated.

In a pie plate or shallow pan, stir together the granulated sugar and remaining 1 teaspoon nutmeg.

Drop the batter into the plate by tablespoon-sized scoops, and use your hands to gently roll the scoops into round shapes in the sugar mixture, turning to coat each scoop thoroughly. (You will probably only have room to roll 6 scoops at a time.) Place each sugared ball on the prepared baking sheets, leaving about 2 inches between cookies (these will flatten and spread during baking). Bake for 11 to 13 minutes, until the cookies have spread and just begin to brown at the edges. (They may not look done in the centers when they are removed from the oven, but they will firm as they cool.) Leave the cookies on the baking sheets for about 3 minutes after removing them from the oven, then use a metal spatula to transfer them to a wire rack to cool.

The cookies can be stored for up to 2 weeks in an airtight container at room temperature, or they can be frozen in a zippered, freezer-strength plastic bag for up to 6 months.

THE SHAD ARE RUNNING, PEEPERS ARE JUST BEGINNING TO SING,
THE MAPLES WEAR A VEIL OF DELICATE RED BLOSSOMS,
THERE'S A FAT ROBIN ON THE GREENING LAWN,
AND EVERY RAIN SHOWER BRINGS MORE DELICATE COLOR
TO THE ROADSIDE AND GARDEN.

sautéed shad roe
page No. 85

steamed fiddlehead ferns
page No. 86

jazzy brown rice
page No. 87

lemon pudding cake
page No. 88

sautéed shad roe

***

SERVES 6

**When Connecticut River shad and the egg sacs (shad roe)
turn up in fish markets in late March and
early April, New Englanders know that even though there
might be frost at night, spring is around the corner.
I find the shad itself to be too bony to be worth the time and effort,
but the roe is a different kettle of fish, as it were.
A simple preparation and patience are the keys to making it
look and taste as wonderful as it can be.
Shad roe is very rich, so small servings are advised—use warmed
salad plates so the entrée doesn't get lost on the plate.**

3 pairs shad roe, separated
(see note)

Salt and freshly ground
black pepper

½ cup (2.5 ounces) unbleached
all-purpose flour

2 tablespoons fine-grind cornmeal

About ¾ cup (1½ sticks; 6 ounces)
unsalted butter, or more
if necessary

2 to 3 tablespoons fresh lemon juice

1 tablespoon Worcestershire sauce

⅓ cup chopped fresh flat-leaf
(Italian) parsley leaves

12 slices bacon, sautéed until crisp
and crumbled

Carefully wash the roe sacs and dry them gently with paper towels, keeping each sac intact. Sprinkle with salt and pepper to taste. Mix the flour and cornmeal together in a shallow bowl. Dip in the roe sacs to cover each side, gently shaking off any excess.

Place ½ cup of the butter in a heavy skillet just large enough to hold the pairs of roe sacs and cook over medium-high heat until it has melted and foam has subsided. Lower the heat to medium-low, slide in the roe sacs, and cook for 6 to 7 minutes on each side, taking care to regulate the flame so the roe sacs don't burst, until evenly browned. Add more butter if necessary; there should be enough butter in the pan so the bottom side of the roe is completely submerged.

Carefully transfer the roe to heated plates. Add the lemon juice, Worcestershire sauce, parsley, and any remaining butter to the skillet and whisk until the butter melts, then pour the juices over the roe. Sprinkle on the crumbled bacon and serve immediately.

NOTE: Shad roe sacs are found in pairs; each elongated sac holds thousands of eggs and is surrounded by a transparent, fairly resilient membrane. Separate the roe sacs in each pair gently, taking care not to rupture the membrane.

steamed fiddlehead ferns

1½ pounds fresh fiddlehead ferns

2 to 3 tablespoons mild olive oil

1 tablespoon balsamic vinegar

1 tablespoon soy sauce

1 teaspoon finely grated lemon zest

Freshly ground black pepper

**This is one vegetable that is so delicate in flavor,
the less done to it the better. You can pick your own,
or you might be lucky enough to find them in a farmers' market
or even in the vegetable section of your supermarket.
When you see them, grab them, because the season is so short
you won't find them again until next year.
The ferns should be bright green and tightly closed.
If they have brown ends, trim them off before cooking.**

Trim any dry, brown ends from the fiddleheads and place them in a bowl of cold water to soak for 15 to 20 minutes. Drain well. Place in a steamer basket set in a saucepan and add cold water to a depth of 1 inch. Cover the pan, bring the water to a simmer, and steam the fiddleheads until just tender, 6 to 7 minutes. The cooking time will depend on the size of the fiddleheads and the size of the steamer.

Transfer the fiddleheads to a serving bowl and drizzle over the olive oil, vinegar, soy sauce, and zest. Sprinkle with pepper to taste and serve hot or at room temperature.

jazzy brown rice

***

SERVES 8

**Using a rice cooker to make brown (and also, of course, white)
rice will eliminate the soggy, overcooked results that
can happen when you boil brown rice in a pan on the stove.
This side dish, which sparkles with flavor and shines with color,
could become a main course with the addition
of shredded cooked chicken or small cubes of tofu.**

4 cups (20 ounces) cooked brown rice (prepared without salt), warm or at room temperature

1 cup (4 ounces) shelled, toasted pistachio nuts

½ cup (2 ounces) dried apricots, chopped

Freshly grated zest of 1 orange

¾ teaspoon ground cinnamon

3 tablespoons vegetable oil

1 small yellow onion, peeled and diced

Sea salt and freshly ground black pepper

Combine the rice, pistachio nuts, apricots, orange zest, and cinnamon in a large serving bowl. Stir gently with a wooden spoon to combine.

Heat 1 tablespoon of the oil in a small sauté pan or skillet over medium-low heat. Add the onion and sauté until translucent, about 5 minutes. Stir the onion into the rice mixture. Sprinkle the mixture with the remaining 2 tablespoons oil and season with salt and pepper to taste. Toss gently and serve warm or at room temperature.

lemon pudding cake

***

4 tablespoons (½ stick; 2 ounces) unsalted butter, at room temperature

¾ cup (6 ounces) plus 2 tablespoons granulated sugar

⅓ cup (1.67 ounces) unbleached all-purpose flour

¼ teaspoon salt

4 extra-large eggs, separated, at room temperature

Finely grated zest of 2 large lemons

½ cup (4 ounces) strained freshly squeezed lemon juice

1 cup whole milk

This traditional and very splendid recipe will bring many of you back to your grandmother's kitchen. *Light* and *lemony* are the watchwords of this homey cake that makes its own velvety sauce as it bakes. Served warm from the oven, or even at room temperature, it's a perfect ending to a memorable meal.

Preheat the oven to 325°F with the rack in the center position. Put a kettle of water on to boil. Use 1 tablespoon of the butter to grease an 8-inch square baking pan. Sprinkle the 2 tablespoons sugar in the greased pan and tilt the pan to coat the bottom and sides. Let the excess sugar stay on the bottom of the pan, evenly distributed. Set aside. Have ready a roasting pan large enough to accommodate the baking pan without its sides touching the roasting pan.

Put the remaining 3 tablespoons butter, the ¾ cup sugar, the flour, and the salt in the work bowl of a food processor and pulse several times to combine. Add the egg yolks and lemon zest and process until smooth. Scrape down the sides of the bowl, then, with the machine running, slowly add the lemon juice and then the milk. Process until the mixture is very smooth. Set aside.

With a stand mixer or handheld electric mixer with spotlessly clean beaters and in a clean bowl, beat the egg whites until stiff, but not dry, peaks form. Carefully pour the yolk mixture into the whites, then fold gently until you can no longer see large areas of egg white. (There will be small pockets of whites throughout.) Ladle or pour the batter into the prepared baking pan. Place the baking pan in the roasting pan and place both in the oven. Carefully pour boiling water into the roasting pan so that the water comes halfway up the sides of the baking pan. Bake for 30 to 35 minutes, or until the top is golden brown in places (it won't brown evenly) and the cake feels firm when touched. Turn off the oven and open the oven door. Leave the cake in the oven, in its water bath, for 5 minutes. Carefully remove both pans from the oven and transfer the baking pan to a wire rack to cool slightly. Serve warm.

NOTE: While the cake is best when served warm, it may be served at room temperature. It should not be refrigerated.

IS IT SOMETHING IN THE AIR, SOMETHING IN THE WATER,
OR IS LITCHFIELD COUNTY SIMPLY
A MAGNET FOR TALENTED FOLKS WITH GREEN THUMBS?
DINNER IN THE GARDEN IN ITS FULL GLORY
(OR ON A SCREENED-IN PORCH IF MOSQUITOES ARE AN ISSUE)
IS ONE OF THE HIGHLIGHTS OF SUMMER.

prosecco and fraises des bois

cheese snaps

cold poached chicken breasts with champagne sauce

roasted vegetables

bulgur salad with fresh herbs

pavés d'or

prosecco and fraises des bois

***

SERVES 8

Prosecco is a fizzy Italian wine with a delicate aroma and taste that has been compared to summer flowers. While you can make this aperitif with any sparkling wine and regular strawberries, the called-for ingredients make it so special that the word *dazzling* comes to mind. Fraises des bois are tiny, intensely flavored strawberries that are so fragile they are (in most cases) sold close to where they are grown. They are, in fact, easy to grow, so if you develop a fondness for this libation, you may wish to grow your own.

½ pint fraises des bois or very small, flavorful strawberries

Two 750-ml bottles Prosecco, well chilled

Fresh mint sprigs for garnish

Place a few berries in the bottom of each of 8 Champagne flutes or wineglasses. Fill the glasses with Prosecco and garnish with fresh mint. Serve immediately.

cheese snaps

1 cup (2 sticks; 8 ounces) unsalted butter, at room temperature

12 ounces smoked Gouda cheese, grated

4 ounces Gruyère cheese, grated

1½ teaspoons salt

½ teaspoon paprika

¼ teaspoon cayenne pepper, or more to taste

3 cups (15 ounces) unbleached all-purpose flour

1 tablespoon baking powder

"Savory shortbread" is the description that springs to mind when I nibble one (or two, or twelve) of these completely irresistible crackers. When you serve them, you don't have to bother with the ubiquitous cheese platter— these are an all-in-one-bite tidbit to serve with drinks.

Preheat the oven to 350°F with 2 racks placed as close to the center of the oven as possible. Line 2 baking sheets with parchment paper, aluminum foil, or silicone pan liners.

In a food processor, process the butter, Gouda, Gruyère, salt, paprika, and cayenne until the mixture is creamy. Add the flour and baking powder and pulse until smooth.

Turn the dough onto a floured surface and, with lightly floured hands, pinch off walnut-sized pieces of the dough. Shape each piece into a ball and place the balls on the prepared baking sheets, leaving 1½ inches between the balls. Dip the tines of a fork into flour and use the back of the fork to press each ball into a flat disk about ¼ inch thick. Press the fork into the disks in the crosswise direction to create a crosshatch pattern on each disk.

Bake the crackers until they are lightly golden on the bottom and edges, 20 to 22 minutes. Transfer the baking sheets to wire racks and let the crackers cool on the baking sheets. Serve as soon as they are cool enough to eat, or store in an airtight container at room temperature for up to 3 days.

cold poached chicken breasts with champagne sauce

***

SERVES 8

If the idea of using Champagne in a sauce surprises you, think about all the times you've added white wine to a dish to give it that special accent that broth or stock alone can't deliver. You can use almost any Champagne—brut (dry) or sec (sweet)— as long as it's not super sweet. The best plan is to ask your favorite wine merchant for direction. You don't need to spend a lot, either—make sure you tell the person advising you that it's for cooking (although there is certainly enough left over in a whole bottle for the cook to have a glass as well).

4 skinless, boneless whole chicken breasts, halved

2½ cups (20 ounces) canned low-sodium chicken broth

2½ cups (20 ounces) Champagne or other dry sparkling white wine

3 whole fresh sage leaves

2½ cups (20 ounces) heavy cream

Salt

1 tablespoon pink peppercorns, ground in a spice grinder or with a mortar and pestle

1 tablespoon freshly chopped sage leaves

Place the chicken breast pieces in a 3-quart saucepan and pour in the broth and Champagne. Add the whole sage leaves and bring to a gentle simmer over medium-low heat. Reduce the heat to low and continue simmering, covered, for 20 minutes, or until the chicken breasts are opaque throughout. Remove the chicken from the pot with a slotted spoon, reserving the poaching liquid. Refrigerate the chicken in a covered container while you make the sauce. (Both the chicken and poaching liquid can be prepared up to 2 days ahead and refrigerated, covered, in separate containers.)

Discard the sage leaves from the poaching liquid and bring the liquid to a boil over high heat. Cook until the liquid is reduced to 2½ cups, about 30 minutes. Add the heavy cream and cook over medium-high heat until the liquid is reduced again to 3 cups, about 20 to 25 more minutes. (Be attentive; as the sauce boils the cream may sputter a bit.) Remove from the heat. Season the sauce to taste with salt and add the pink peppercorns and the chopped sage. Refrigerate in a covered container until well chilled.

To serve, cut each cold breast in half crosswise, on the diagonal, into 5 to 6 slices and fan the slices out on each of 8 dinner plates. Nap the slices with a small amount of chilled sauce. Pass the remaining sauce on the side.

COLD POACHED CHICKEN BREASTS WITH CHAMPAGNE SAUCE

see page No. 93

ROASTED VEGETABLES

see page N°. 96

roasted vegetables

4 small turnips, peeled and quartered lengthwise

8 carrots, peeled and cut on the diagonal into 2-inch lengths

16 whole Brussels sprouts, trimmed

4 shallots, peeled and halved

2 large golden beets, blanched, peeled, and quartered

4 parsnips, peeled and cut on the diagonal into 2-inch lengths

2 yams, peeled and quartered

3 tablespoons mild olive oil

3 tablespoons canola oil

1 tablespoon balsamic vinegar

2 tablespoons coarse salt

1 tablespoon finely chopped fresh sage leaves

Freshly ground black pepper

The natural sugar in root vegetables caramelizes during roasting, turning each bite into a flavor burst. Done correctly, the vegetables have a tender interior and a slightly crunchy crust.

Preheat the oven to 425°F with 2 racks placed as close to the center of the oven as possible.

In a large bowl, combine the turnips, carrots, Brussels sprouts, shallots, beets, parsnips, and yams and toss to combine. Drizzle them with the olive and canola oils, vinegar, salt, sage, and black pepper to taste and toss with a wooden spoon until the vegetables are evenly coated. Place the vegetables in a single layer on 2 large, rimmed baking sheets. (Using 2 baking sheets is best, so that the vegetables can roast in a single layer. You want to be sure that they caramelize as they roast rather than steam.)

Roast, testing occasionally with a skewer or the tines of a fork, until the vegetables are tender but not mushy, about 1 hour. Stir the vegetables gently every 20 minutes to ensure even browning. Serve hot or at room temperature.

bulgur salad with fresh herbs

***

SERVES 8

If you are a fan of tabbouleh, you are familiar with bulgur (also known as *bulghur*), a quick-cooking form of whole wheat that has been cleaned, parboiled, and ground into various sizes. Bulgur has the same lovely sweet, nutty taste that is found in whole-wheat bread, and is equally nutritious. Because the bran—the part of the wheat that contains the oil—has been removed, bulgur is shelf-stable for quite a long time because there is little or no oil to become rancid.

This salad can be made up to 48 hours before serving and stored in a covered container in the refrigerator.

1 head roasted garlic (see note)

1 cup (3.5 ounces) bulgur

1¼ teaspoons salt, plus more to taste

1¼ cups (10 ounces) vegetable broth

¼ cup (2 ounces) fresh lemon juice

¼ cup (2 ounces) mild olive oil

½ cup fresh flat-leaf (Italian) parsley leaves, minced

¼ cup fresh mint leaves, minced

2 tablespoons minced fresh chives

One 13½-ounce can chickpeas, drained

½ cup (4 ounces) crumbled feta cheese

10 cherry tomatoes, halved

Freshly ground black pepper

Remove the roasted garlic from the cloves by squeezing the base of each clove until the garlic is released. Mash the garlic with a fork and set aside.

Place the bulgur and 1¼ teaspoons salt in a large, heatproof serving bowl. In a medium saucepan, bring the broth just to a gentle boil over medium heat. Remove from the heat and pour the broth over the bulgur. Stir well, cover, and let stand for 15 to 20 minutes or until the liquid is absorbed and the bulgur has softened. Add the lemon juice and olive oil and toss well to distribute the ingredients evenly. Add the mashed garlic; stir well to distribute the roasted garlic evenly. Add the parsley, mint, chives, chickpeas, and feta; toss well to combine. Cover with plastic wrap and refrigerate for at least 3 to 4 hours to allow the flavors to develop.

Immediately before serving, add the cherry tomatoes. Season with pepper and additional salt, if desired, and serve.

CONT'D

NOTE: To roast a head of garlic, preheat the oven to 325°F with the rack in the center position. Turn the head of garlic on its side and cut off the top portion of the papery skin with a sharp knife. The uppermost part of each clove should be exposed. Place the garlic in a small ramekin. Drizzle 1 tablespoon of olive oil and ½ teaspoon of salt over the garlic. Cover with foil and roast for about 45 minutes, or until the garlic is golden brown and tender when pierced with the tip of a sharp knife. Carefully remove the foil and allow the garlic to cool in the oil to room temperature.

pavés d'or

These gold-dusted chocolate diamonds melt in the mouth and remind us why the best part of the meal comes last. This special dessert may inspire you to skip dinner and go straight for the gold. The base is a flourless chocolate cake that seems to say "I spent all day on this," when in fact, start to finish, it should take no more than an hour, including baking. It's very important here to use the very best chocolate you can find—never chocolate chips—since the taste of the chocolate is what paves its way to your happy mouth. The other thing you might consider using is one of the ultra-high-fat sweet (unsalted) butters (either domestic or imported) that are now available in grocery and specialty-food stores.

8 ounces unsweetened chocolate, roughly chopped

4 ounces bittersweet chocolate, roughly chopped

1 cup (2 sticks; 8 ounces) unsalted butter, at room temperature, cut into small pieces

5 extra-large eggs, at room temperature

½ cup (4 ounces) water

1⅓ cups (10.25 ounces) granulated sugar

2 tablespoons edible gold dust or gold leaf (see note)

Preheat the oven to 350°F with the rack in the center position. Butter an 8-inch square baking pan. Line the pan with two 8-inch-wide lengths of parchment, placed perpendicular to each other, and long enough so that the ends extend beyond the sides of the pan. Butter the parchment that lines the bottom and sides of the pan. Have ready a baking pan large enough to hold the 8-inch square pan. Bring a pot of water to a boil.

Put the unsweetened and bittersweet chocolates in the bowl of a food processor fitted with the steel blade and process until they are in tiny pieces.

Have the butter ready at the work area and break the eggs into a small bowl. Combine the water with the sugar in a small saucepan and bring the mixture to a rolling boil. When the sugar mixture is boiling, turn on the processor and pour the boiling mixture over the chocolate. Leave the processor on and add the butter, piece by piece, then pour in the eggs. Process until the mixture is very smooth. Pour the batter into the prepared pan and set it in the larger pan. Place both pans in the oven and carefully pour hot water into the larger pan, making sure not to add water to the batter in the smaller pan.

CONT'D

Bake for about 30 minutes, until the cake is set and just a bit of fudgy batter clings to a cake tester inserted in the center of the cake. The top will still look wet and shiny. Remove the pans from the oven and carefully remove the smaller pan from the larger one. Let the cake cool in the pan on a wire rack.

When the cake is cool, place a piece of parchment over the top of the cake and invert the cake onto a cutting board or cookie sheet. Remove the lining parchment from the bottom of the cake and place a cutting board over the cake bottom. Invert the cake again so that it is right side up on the cutting board.

Place the gold dust in a small sieve and gently sift the gold dust over the cake, or apply a tiny bit of gold leaf to the top of the cake. Cut the cake into 1-inch-wide lengths, then cut each length diagonally into diamonds. Transfer the diamonds as they are cut to small paper cups (like candy cups). Store them in an airtight container in the refrigerator until 1 hour before serving.

NOTE: Edible gold dust and leaf can be ordered online through the King Arthur Flour Baker's Catalogue, www.kingarthurflour.com, 800-827-6836; at www.misterart.com; or at www.goldleafcompany.com.

Rhode Island

The smallest state in size only, **Rhode Island** is packed with exciting, beautiful, and interesting experiences in practically every square foot. The food, with its **Portuguese** and **Italian** influences, is big and bold and full of flavor—just like the spirit of the state itself.

O.K., SO YOUR SHIP HASN'T COME IN...YET.
BUT YOU CAN DREAM.
MEANWHILE, SECURE THE LINES, BATTEN DOWN
THE HATCHES, PULL UP A DECK CHAIR,
AND ENJOY THIS BREAKFAST THAT IS EQUALLY TASTY
WHETHER YOU ARE ON LAND OR AT SEA.

clam digger

***

SERVES 2

**I like to think of this as a New (and Better) Age Bloody Mary.
As a variation, go a step further than serving this drink
in a traditional highball glass: Make clam (or oyster) shooters
by placing a small raw clam (such as a cherrystone) or oyster
in the bottom of each of four 2-ounce shot glasses and
pouring the premixed drink ingredients over it.
Don't forget to warn your guests that the clam lurks in
the bottom of the glass . . . you wouldn't want to be called on
to perform the Heimlich maneuver.**

2 ounces tequila

3 ounces regular or spicy V8 Juice

3 ounces bottled clam juice

2 teaspoons prepared horseradish

2 tablespoons fresh lime juice

Splash of Worcestershire sauce

A few drops of Tabasco or other hot-pepper sauce (optional)

Fresh celery stalks for garnish

Shake the tequila, V8 juice, clam juice, horseradish, lime juice, and
Worcestershire sauce in a cocktail shaker. Fill two highball glasses
halfway with ice, pour in the contents of the shaker, and add Tabasco
to taste, if desired. Garnish with celery stalks.

grapefruit and avocado salad

***

SERVES 8

**Refreshing, simple, and pretty on the plate—what more
could you ask for in a summery starter course?**

2 tablespoons mild olive oil

1 tablespoon balsamic vinegar

1 teaspoon soy sauce

3 large pink or red grapefruits, peeled, white pith removed, seeded, and cut into sections

2 ripe avocados, pitted, peeled, and cut into ½-inch wedges

1 medium red onion, cut into ¼-inch dice

¼ pound smoked turkey or ham, cut into ¼-inch dice

Whisk together the oil, vinegar, and soy sauce in a small, nonreactive
bowl. Put the grapefruit and avocado in a medium, nonreactive bowl
and toss to combine. Add the onion and turkey and toss gently to
combine. Pour on the dressing, stir gently, and serve immediately.

If you like, the salad—without the avocado—can be made up to
12 hours ahead and refrigerated in a covered container. Prepare and
add the avocado just before serving.

johnny cake

***

MAKES 1 LOAF

1 cup (5 ounces) fine-grind white cornmeal

¾ cup (3.75 ounces) unbleached all-purpose flour

¼ cup (2 ounces) granulated sugar

2½ teaspoons baking powder

¾ teaspoon salt

1¾ cups (10 ounces) fresh white corn kernels cut from the cob (3 large ears) or frozen kernels, thawed and drained

2 extra-large eggs

1 cup (8 ounces) whole milk

¼ cup (½ stick; 2 ounces) unsalted butter, melted and cooled

To get authentic Johnny Cake "flour" (white cornmeal), you really should come to Rhode Island, where Kenyon's Grist Mill in West Kingston, grinds its own white corn in a mill built in 1886 and purchased by Charles Kenyon in 1906.

This is not the traditional pancake form, but a moist loaf that contains white cornmeal and white corn kernels. Frozen white corn kernels are found in most supermarkets with the other frozen vegetables; you can order white cornmeal from Kenyon's Grist Mill, www.kenyonsgristmill.com, 401-783-4054. Yellow cornmeal and yellow corn kernels may be substituted for the white in this recipe.

My favorite way to eat this is spread with a generous amount of sweet (unsalted) butter. It makes great toast, but use the toaster oven for this job, as the slices are a bit too crumbly for a conventional toaster.

Preheat the oven to 400°F with the rack at the center position. Butter and flour an 8½-by-4½-by-2½-inch loaf pan; set aside.

In a large bowl whisk together the cornmeal, flour, sugar, baking powder, and salt. Toss ¾ cup of the corn kernels in the flour mixture; set aside.

Put the remaining 1 cup corn kernels, the eggs, milk, and melted butter in the work bowl of a food processor fitted with the metal blade. Process until the mixture is fairly smooth with small flecks of corn remaining, 15 to 20 seconds. Pour the egg mixture into the flour mixture. Stir just until combined, with no flour pockets remaining. Scrape the mixture into the prepared pan.

Bake until the loaf is lightly browned, has started to come away from the sides of the pan, and a cake tester inserted in the middle of the loaf comes out almost clean, 45 to 50 minutes. Transfer to a wire rack and let the loaf cool completely in the pan (otherwise the center will be underbaked). When completely cool, remove the loaf from the pan and slice.

The loaf can be stored, wrapped in aluminum foil, at room temperature for 2 days, or in the refrigerator for up to 6 days.

frittata soufflé

***

SERVES 6 TO 8

Folding beaten egg whites into this frittata doesn't really turn it into a traditional soufflé, but it does give it a light, airy texture that is just the ticket when you are looking for a substantial, but not overly filling, first meal of the day. It's great hot from the oven, but equally delicious at room temperature.

2 tablespoons (1 ounce) unsalted butter

1 medium potato, peeled and thinly sliced

8 green onions, white parts only, thinly sliced

2 cloves garlic, peeled and minced

1 cup cooked spinach, squeezed well to remove moisture (either frozen and defrosted or made by steaming 1 large bunch fresh spinach leaves)

8 extra-large eggs, separated

½ cup (4 ounces) light cream

½ teaspoon dried thyme, or 2 teaspoons fresh thyme leaves

½ teaspoon kosher salt

½ cup (4 ounces) crumbled goat cheese

Preheat the oven to 425°F with the rack in the center position. Melt the butter in a large, ovenproof skillet. Add the potato slices and sauté until golden brown, about 10 minutes. Add the green onions and garlic and cook for 1 minute. Add the spinach and mix well. Cook until the spinach is heated through. Remove from the heat.

Put the egg yolks in a medium bowl. Add the cream, thyme, and salt; mix well. Mix in the crumbled goat cheese. In a large mixing bowl, beat the egg whites until they are stiff but not dry. Gently fold the egg yolk mixture into the whites until there are no streaks of white left. Pour the egg mixture onto the vegetables in the skillet and, using just a few gentle strokes, fold the vegetables into the eggs. Smooth the top. Bake until puffed and brown, 30 to 35 minutes. Cut into wedges and serve hot or at room temperature.

stilton cheesecake

SERVES 12 AS AN APPETIZER

When I first created this savory cheesecake many years ago, the concept of blue-cheese cheesecake was hard for people to get their minds around—until they tasted the first bite. After that they wondered, along with me, why no one had thought of the idea before.

The secret to getting a cheesecake—whether sweet or savory—to bake with a smooth top is to prepare it in the food processor, not with a mixer, which beats air into the batter. The air bubbles expand during baking, causing the cheesecake to rise. Unable to sustain the weight, it falls and cracks upon cooling.

¼ cup (1.25 ounces) fine dried bread crumbs

½ cup (2 ounces) freshly grated Parmesan cheese

3 tablespoons (1½ ounces) unsalted butter

2 shallots, peeled and finely diced

½ pound (8 ounces) Stilton or other blue-veined cheese, crumbled

1¾ pounds (28 ounces) regular cream cheese (not reduced fat), at room temperature

4 extra-large eggs

⅓ cup (2.7 ounces) heavy cream

A few drops of Tabasco or other hot-pepper sauce

½ pound thick-cut bacon, cut into small dice and cooked until very crisp

Salad greens tossed with the dressing of your choice for serving

Preheat the oven to 300°F with the rack in the center position. Generously butter the bottom and sides of an 8-inch springform pan with 3-inch sides. Line the bottom with a circle of parchment paper; butter the parchment. Mix the bread crumbs together with ¼ cup of the Parmesan cheese. Dust the interior of the pan with the bread-crumb mixture, allowing the excess to stay evenly distributed on the bottom of the pan. This cheesecake cooks in a water bath; to prevent water from leaking into the pan while the cheesecake bakes, place it on a 16-inch length of heavy-duty aluminum foil, gather the edges up, and wrap them around the outside of the springform, securing if necessary with a length of kitchen string tied around the outside of the pan.

Have ready a roasting pan large enough to hold the prepared spring-form pan. Bring a large pot of water to a boil.

Melt the 3 tablespoons butter in a small skillet set over medium heat. Add the shallots and cook, stirring frequently, for about 10 minutes, or until the shallots are wilted and translucent. Set aside.

Combine the Stilton cheese, cream cheese, eggs, heavy cream, and Tabasco to taste in the work bowl of a food processor fitted with the metal blade and process until the mixture is completely smooth, stopping to scrape down the sides of the work bowl once or twice. Add the cooked shallots and bacon and pulse to blend, but avoid overprocessing, as you want the bacon to create some texture in the batter.

Pour and scrape the mixture into the prepared pan. Sprinkle the remaining ¼ cup Parmesan cheese on top. Place the springform pan in the larger roasting pan and set both in the oven. Add enough boiling water to come halfway up the sides of the springform pan. Bake the cheesecake for 1 hour and 40 minutes, checking the water bath halfway through the cooking time; add more, if necessary. At the end of the cooking time, turn off the oven and leave the door closed with the cheesecake inside. After 1 hour remove both pans, remove the foil wrapping, dry the bottom of the springform pan, and place it on a wire rack to cool completely. Do not refrigerate the cheesecake to speed the cooling process.

When the cheesecake is cool, release the sides of the pan and slide a wide metal spatula under the cake to transfer it to a serving platter. (You may opt to serve it right on the springform pan bottom. If you do, don't use a metal knife to cut the cheesecake, or you'll ruin the pan bottom and the knife.) Cut the cheesecake by slicing it with a long, thin knife that has been run under hot water and dried before slicing. (The cheesecake is best served without refrigerating it. Refrigeration makes it dense and a bit heavy. You can make it up to 1 day ahead of time and keep it at room temperature, wrapped tightly in plastic wrap.)

To serve, put some dressed salad greens on a small plate and place a wedge of cheesecake next to them.

STILTON CHEESECAKE
see page Nº. 110

MULTISEED CRACKER BREAD
see page NO. 114

multiseed cracker bread

***

SERVES 8

1 cup (5 ounces) unbleached all-purpose flour

1 cup (5 ounces) whole-wheat flour

½ cup (2.5 ounces) rye flour

½ cup (2.5 ounces) fine-grind yellow cornmeal

2 teaspoons salt

1 cup (8 ounces) water, plus more if necessary

2 tablespoons mild olive oil

⅔ cup (2.7 ounces) of mixed seeds such as sesame, poppy, fennel, caraway, and anise

¼ cup of mixed dried herbs such as rosemary, basil, dill, tarragon, and thyme

1 teaspoon freshly ground black pepper

1 tablespoon coarse salt (optional, if you like a salty, crunchy cracker)

The concept of making your own crackers has perhaps never occurred to you. But once you give it a try, you'll be hooked. Here is a case in which the making is almost as much fun as the eating. The crackers are made in large, irregular sheets which can be arranged and served whole, or broken up ahead of time.

Preheat the oven to 450°F with the rack in the center position. Select several heavy-duty baking sheets; turn them over so that you use the undersides. Spray each underside very lightly with nonstick vegetable spray, or cover with a silicone pan liner.

Put the all-purpose flour, whole-wheat flour, rye flour, cornmeal, the 2 teaspoons salt, water, and oil in a bread machine programmed for dough, in the bowl of a stand mixer fitted with the kneading attachment, or in the work bowl of a food processor fitted with the dough blade. Knead, mix, or process until you have achieved a stiff yet supple ball of dough. Add more all-purpose flour if the dough is too wet or more water if it seems too dry. This dough does not require a long kneading period, just enough time to get it to hold together well—and since the dough contains no leavening, it doesn't rise before or during the baking process.

Combine the seeds, herbs, pepper, and coarse salt, if using, in a small bowl. Divide the dough into 8 pieces. Working with 1 piece at a time (keep the others covered with a cloth or plastic wrap), scatter about 1 tablespoon of the seed mixture on the work surface. Press the dough onto the seed mixture and, using a heavy-duty rolling pin, begin to roll it out as thinly as possible. (If you are using a silicone pan liner, it's actually easier to roll the dough out on the liner before placing the liner on the baking sheet.) If the dough sticks, flip it over, apply more of the seed mixture and continue rolling. The goal is to get the dough as thin as possible and impregnated with lots of seeds. You may find it easier to finish the rolling right on the baking sheet. You may be able to fit more than one cracker bread on a sheet. Continue to roll out the dough portions and place them on baking sheets.

As sheets are ready, start baking the cracker breads, one baking sheet at a time. Bake for 4 to 5 minutes, or until the top side is quite brown, then flip the dough over and bake until the other side is equally brown, another 2 to 3 minutes. (At this point you can even take the cracker bread off the baking sheet and bake it right on the oven rack.) When the cracker breads are done, cool completely on wire racks before serving. Serve whole, standing upright (on edge) in a basket, or break into sections.

Store the crackers, uncovered, in a dry place. If the cracker breads get soggy (which they will do during humid weather), they are easily crisped by placing them in a 250°F oven for 10 minutes.

THERE ARE AREAS OF THE RHODE ISLAND SHORE
WHERE THE DAYS BEGIN WITH COOL, MISTY MORNINGS AND
SEGUE INTO BRIGHT, SUNLIT AFTERNOONS.
THIS PATTERN, COMBINED WITH PARTICULARLY FAVORABLE
SOIL CONDITIONS, CREATES A MICROCLIMATE NOT UNLIKE THOSE
OF THE WINE-PRODUCING AREAS OF NORTHERN FRANCE.
LUNCH, PRESENTED ON A TABLE WITH A VIEW OF GRAPE-LADEN VINES,
WOULD BE PERFECT ENJOYED WITH A BOTTLE OF ONE OF
RHODE ISLAND'S AWARD-WINNING VINTAGES.

uncle leo's smoked bluefish spread
page NO. 117

pain de champagne
page NO. 118

tomato and goat cheese salad
page NO. 119

poached salmon with sorrel sauce
page NO. 122

triple-apple crumble
page NO. 124

uncle leo's smoked bluefish spread

***

MAKES ABOUT 1 POUND; SERVES 8 GENEROUSLY

It was my friends Judy and Carl Salzman who first introduced me to their Uncle Leo's (a.k.a. Dr. Leo Salzman) masterpiece. I believe I polished off the entire bowl, leaving only the crackers for the rest of the guests. "It's so ridiculously simple to make," Judy kept insisting when I pressed her for the recipe. And indeed it is. Thanks go out to dear Uncle Leo, who spends his summers catching and smoking bluefish in Truro, Massachusetts. We can't wait for his next brainstorm.

The spread will keep for a week in the refrigerator—but there probably won't be any left over to worry about.

1 pound (16 ounces) meaty smoked bluefish (Uncle Leo strongly suggests there be "no scrawny ends," as there won't be enough oil in the finished pâté), skin removed and fish cut into 1-inch pieces

1 medium onion, peeled and quartered

Freshly ground black pepper

Tabasco or other hot-pepper sauce

Put the bluefish, onion, and pepper and Tabasco to taste in the work bowl of a food processor fitted with the metal blade and pulse until a rough paste forms. Add more pepper and Tabasco, if desired. Scrape the spread into a serving dish, cover tightly with plastic wrap, and refrigerate until ready to serve with crackers or toast.

pain de champagne

For the sponge:

1 cup (8 ounces) brut (dry)
Champagne (leftover,
flat Champagne is fine)

2 teaspoons active dry yeast

1 cup (5 ounces) unbleached
all-purpose flour

For the dough:

1 teaspoon active dry yeast

1 teaspoon salt

4 tablespoons Lora Brody's Dough
Relaxer (optional, for a softer,
richer loaf; see note)

2¼ cups (11.25 ounces)
unbleached all-purpose flour

3 tablespoons unsalted butter,
at room temperature

1 extra-large egg

*We once had a party and hired local college kids
to serve and tend bar. They opened up every bottle of a case of
Champagne, which, needless to say, made me very cross and
left us with a large amount of flat Champagne
to either throw out or get creative with. This unusual loaf is
how I made lemonade out of those proverbial lemons.*

To make the sponge, pour the Champagne into a medium mixing
bowl. Sprinkle on the 2 teaspoons yeast and stir until it dissolves. Stir
in the 1 cup flour. Cover with a clean kitchen towel and leave at room
temperature for 12 hours. The mixture will appear slightly bubbly,
like a sourdough starter that has been fed.

When ready to make the dough, put the yeast, salt, Dough Relaxer
(if using), flour, butter, and egg in a large mixing bowl. Add the
sponge and stir until a soft dough forms. Turn the dough out onto a
lightly floured work surface and knead briefly to form a soft, supple
dough. Put the dough in a well-oiled bowl and let rise until doubled in
bulk. Gently deflate the dough, place it in a well-buttered 8½-by-4½-
by-2½-inch loaf pan, cover, and let rise in a warm place until nearly
doubled in bulk.

Preheat the oven to 400°F with the rack in the center position. Bake
for 40 minutes, or until an instant-read thermometer inserted in the
center registers 200°F and the top is a deep, golden brown. Remove
the loaf from the pan and let cool on a wire rack before slicing.

NOTE: Lora Brody's Dough Relaxer is available at www.lorabrody.com,
888-9-Bakeit; or at the King Arthur Flour Baker's Catalogue,
www.kingarthurflour.com, 800-827-6836.

tomato and goat cheese salad

***

SERVES 6 TO 8

**When locally grown tomatoes are in the market
(or ripe in your own garden), that's the time to think about
making this salad. The marriage of tangy tomatoes,
creamy goat cheese, and the crunch of croutons makes a perfect
start to a summer meal or main course for lunch.**

**Store-bought croutons are a far distant cousin to homemade,
and since it's easy to make your own, there's no excuse not to
crown this lovely salad with the real thing.**

To make the croutons, in a large skillet, heat the olive oil over medium heat. Add the garlic halves and cook, stirring, until they are fragrant but not brown (or, heat the garlic-infused oil in the skillet). Add the bread cubes and stir well to coat with the oil. Sprinkle the cubes with the kosher salt. Continue to cook, stirring and tossing the cubes often, until the cubes are lightly browned and crisp on all sides, about 15 minutes. Set aside to cool while you make the rest of the salad. (The cooled croutons can be stored in an airtight container or plastic bag for up to 1 day.)

To make the dressing, put the mustard, vinegar, and lemon juice in a small bowl. Add the salt and pepper, then add the olive oil drop by drop, whisking vigorously while the oil is being added. Continue to whisk until all the oil is added and the mixture is thickened. Set aside.

In a very large serving bowl combine the tomatoes, cucumbers, bell peppers, basil, mesclun, arugula, and goat cheese. Mix well. Mix in the cooled croutons. Pour the dressing over the salad and mix well. Serve immediately, or allow the salad to rest in the refrigerator for an hour to soften the croutons, if you wish.

For the croutons:

¼ cup (2 ounces) olive oil (you may use ¼ cup garlic-infused olive oil and omit the 2 cloves garlic)

2 cloves garlic, peeled and halved lengthwise

1 small loaf good-quality Italian bread, cut into ½-inch cubes (about 7 cups cubes)

1 teaspoon kosher salt

For the dressing:

½ teaspoon Dijon mustard

2 tablespoons white wine vinegar

1 tablespoon fresh lemon juice

½ teaspoon kosher or sea salt

½ teaspoon freshly ground black pepper

½ cup (4 ounces) extra-virgin olive oil

3 medium, ripe tomatoes, cored and cut into ½-inch pieces

2 large cucumbers, peeled, seeded, and quartered lengthwise, each quarter cut into ½-inch slices

2 red bell peppers, halved lengthwise, seeded, and cut into ½-inch pieces

¼ cup fresh basil leaves, slivered

3 cups mesclun salad greens, washed and well dried

2 cups arugula, washed and well dried

3 ounces soft, mild goat cheese, chilled then crumbled

TOMATO AND GOAT CHEESE SALAD
see page N⁰. 119

POACHED SALMON WITH SORREL SAUCE

see page N°. 122

poached salmon with sorrel sauce

1 lemon

5 garlic cloves, peeled and halved

2 cups (16 ounces) dry white wine

1 cup (8 ounces) fish stock
(see note)

8 large sprigs (½ ounce) fresh dill,
or 2 tablespoons dried dill

1 teaspoon freshly ground
black pepper

One 2-pound salmon fillet,
skin removed

For the Sorrel Sauce:

6 ounces (4 cups) fresh spinach,
well washed

2 ounces (1½ cups) fresh
sorrel leaves

1 cup (8 ounces) plain,
low-fat yogurt

⅓ cup (2.67 ounces) sour cream

½ teaspoon kosher salt

½ teaspoon ground white pepper

1 teaspoon fresh lemon juice

If possible, use wild-caught, as opposed to farm-raised, salmon for this summery recipe. There is a world of difference in the flavor and the texture of the two types of salmon; the latter is so mild its flavor is almost undetectable. The fish and sauce are served cold, so they must be made ahead.

Cut the lemon in half. Squeeze the juice from one half into a large skillet. Slice the other half thinly and set aside. Add the garlic, wine, fish stock, dill, and black pepper to the lemon juice in the pan. Bring to a simmer over medium-high heat. Reduce the heat to low, add the salmon fillet, and cover the salmon with the reserved lemon slices. Cover the pan and cook, adjusting the heat so that the liquid around the salmon barely simmers, for 17 to 20 minutes, until the salmon is opaque throughout.

Remove the salmon from the poaching liquid and place it in a flat container. Cover and refrigerate for at least 2 hours and up to overnight. Strain the poaching liquid into a medium saucepan. Discard the solids and reserve the liquid for making the sorrel sauce.

To make the sauce, heat the reserved poaching liquid to a simmer in the saucepan. Add the spinach and cook over medium heat until the spinach is wilted, 3 to 4 minutes. Use a slotted spoon to transfer the spinach to a colander, and run cold water over the spinach to cool it quickly and stop it from cooking further. Discard the cooking liquid. When cool enough to handle, squeeze the spinach in your hands to remove as much liquid as possible. Put the spinach in the bowl of a food processor. Remove and discard any tough stems from the sorrel leaves and chop the leaves coarsely. Add them to the spinach in the food processor. Add the yogurt, sour cream, salt, and white pepper. Pulse the mixture until the leaves are finely chopped and the yogurt and sour cream are well mixed. Add the lemon juice; pulse to blend. Transfer the sauce to a serving bowl, cover with plastic wrap, and refrigerate.

Serve the salmon with the sorrel sauce on the side.

triple-apple crumble

***

SERVES 8 TO 10

**Apples in three preparations combine to make
this homey dessert a truly special event.
If you haven't ever made homemade applesauce,
you'll be hooked when you see how easy it is and how marvelous
the results are. This is blue-ribbon county-fair cooking
at its best, and you'll find that members of every generation will
want to know exactly when dessert will be served.**

**Use tart, firm, flavorful apples such as
Granny Smith in this recipe.**

6 firm, flavorful apples
(about 3 pounds)

⅓ cup (1.4 ounces) chopped
candied ginger (see notes)

2 tablespoons (1 ounce) unsalted
butter, melted

1½ cups (12 ounces) hard
apple cider

1 tablespoon peeled and grated
fresh gingerroot (see notes)

1¼ cups (5 ounces) dried apple
rings, cut into ½-inch pieces
(see notes)

Finely grated zest of 1 large lemon
(see notes)

½ cup (4 ounces) firmly packed
light brown sugar

For the topping:

7 ounces ginger snaps
(approximately forty 1¾-inch
cookies), ground to coarse crumbs
in a food processor

3 ounces almond biscotti, broken in
several pieces and ground to coarse
crumbs in a food processor

6 tablespoons (3 ounces) unsalted
butter, melted

Best-quality vanilla ice cream
for serving

Preheat the oven to 350°F with the rack in the center position. Have ready a deep-dish pie plate that is about 10 inches in diameter and at least 1½ inches deep.

Peel the apples, cut them in quarters, and cut out the core and seeds. Cut the apples into ½-inch wedges. Scatter half of them in the bottom of the pie plate. Scatter the candied ginger over the apples in the pie plate and drizzle with the melted butter.

Put the remaining apple pieces in a small saucepan. Add ½ cup of the cider and the fresh gingerroot to the apples in the saucepan. Cover and cook over medium heat until the apples are very soft. Let the apples cool in the cooking liquid for several minutes, then purée them in a food processor or with a food mill. (The applesauce may also be made in the microwave: Place the half portion of apples, ½ cup of cider, and the fresh gingerroot in a microwave-safe bowl, microwave on high for 4 to 6 minutes, then let cool slightly.) Spoon the cooled applesauce over the fresh apples in the pie plate and smooth evenly with a rubber spatula.

Put the dried apple ring pieces in a small saucepan (you may use the one that the applesauce cooked in; no need to wash it) over medium-low heat, along with the remaining 1 cup cider, the lemon zest, and the brown sugar. Cover the pan and bring to a simmer. Cook, covered, for about 10 minutes, until almost all the liquid is absorbed. Spoon the cooked dried apples and any cooking liquid over the applesauce, mounding them slightly higher in the center.

To make the topping, toss the ginger snap crumbs and the biscotti crumbs with the melted butter, then sprinkle the mixture over the contents of the pie plate, pressing lightly with your fingers to make the crumbs stick.

Bake the crumble for 45 minutes, or until the top is deep golden brown and the juices are bubbling around the edges. Serve hot from the oven, or warm with a generous scoop of vanilla ice cream.

NOTE: The easiest way to cut dried apples and candied ginger is with a pair of scissors lightly coated with nonstick vegetable spray.

NOTE: A microplane grater is great for grating fresh gingerroot and removing zest from citrus fruits.

A TWILIGHT TOUR OF COLLEGE HILL IN PROVIDENCE
WILL FIND YOU MEANDERING UP COBBLESTONE-LINED STREETS
CALLED ANGEL, BENEFIT, AND HOPE.
TALL WINDOWS OF STATELY BROWNSTONE MANSIONS AND
GRACEFUL VICTORIANS EMIT A WARM, GOLDEN GLOW
WHILE CAST-IRON STREET LANTERNS LIGHT YOUR WAY
PAST LOVINGLY TENDED GARDENS AND PERFECTLY RESTORED
ANTIQUE COLONIAL HOMES. IT'S EASY TO IMAGINE
THE PEOPLE INSIDE ENJOYING DISHES JUST LIKE THESE.

rose-colored glasses

hot artichoke and crab spread

butter lettuce salad with roasted pears and spicy honey-glazed walnuts

indian-spiced braised lamb shanks

chocolate meringue tart

rose-colored glasses

***

SERVES 1

**Many libations that purport to be martinis
have as much in common with the classic drink
as a carnation does with an orchid.
I make no such claims with this recipe—
but I do promise that everything does indeed look better
through rose-colored glasses.**

**Some say Campari is an acquired taste.
This cunning concoction is a good way to start
the acquisition process.**

¾ ounce cranberry vodka

1 ounce cranberry juice

¾ ounce Campari

2 to 3 dried cranberries, plumped
(see note)

Pour the vodka, cranberry juice, and Campari into an ice-filled
martini shaker. Shake well and strain into a very well-chilled martini
glass. Add the cranberries and serve immediately.

NOTE: To plump the cranberries, place them in a small microwave-
safe bowl or 1-cup Pyrex measure. Add enough vodka to cover
them, cover the bowl with plastic wrap, and microwave on high for
1 minute, or until the mixture feels hot to the touch. Allow the
cranberries to cool to warm before removing.

hot artichoke and crab spread

Two 14-ounce cans water-packed
artichokes, drained and
finely chopped

One 6-ounce can crabmeat, drained
and picked over to remove cartilage

1 clove garlic, peeled and
finely minced

1 cup (8 ounces) good-quality
mayonnaise

1 cup (4½ ounces) grated
mozzarella cheese

1 cup (4½ ounces) grated
Parmesan cheese

½ teaspoon Worcestershire sauce

Dash of Tabasco or other
hot-pepper sauce

There are two simple reasons this recipe has endured:
It's very easy to make, and everyone loves it.
Like the martini, it never went away but lingered on the list
of truly scrumptious but near-forgotten indulgences
until a deserving audience came back along.
And while hostesses no longer pass hand-embroidered,
monogrammed cocktail napkins when they serve it and
modernists may scoff and turn up their noses,
I say, make a double recipe!
Even the naysayers will demand a second helping.

Preheat the oven to 350°F with the rack in the center position.
Choose a shallow, decorative baking or gratin dish with at least a
5-cup capacity in which you will both bake and serve the dip. Butter
the interior of the dish. Set aside.

In a large bowl, mix together the artichokes, crabmeat, garlic, mayonnaise, mozzarella cheese, Parmesan cheese, Worcestershire sauce, and
Tabasco. Spoon the mixture into the prepared baking dish and bake
for 20 to 25 minutes, until golden brown and bubbling. Serve hot or
warm with crackers or thinly sliced baguettes.

butter lettuce salad with roasted pears and spicy honey-glazed walnuts

***

SERVES 6

Butter lettuce might be called bibb, Boston, or limestone lettuce at your market. The soft, sweet, pale green leaves make a perfect companion for succulent pears and sweet and spicy walnuts. Fair warning to the cook: You'll sample one nut to see how it tastes, then another, then another . . . so make a few extra.

Preheat the oven to 425°F with the rack in the center position. Peel the pears, cut them in half lengthwise, and remove the cores. Place the pears, cored sides up, in a baking dish just large enough to hold them. Put the water in the bottom of the dish. Dot each pear half with one small piece of butter and sprinkle them with the lemon juice. Cover the dish with aluminum foil and roast the pears for 35 to 45 minutes, turning once halfway through the cooking time. The pears are done when they are tender when pierced with a skewer, but they should not be so soft that they are mushy or lose their shape. Use a large spoon to transfer the pears to a wire rack and allow to cool. When cool, wrap them in plastic wrap or put them in an airtight container and refrigerate them for at least 1 hour and up to 24 hours.

To make the walnuts, heat the butter in a medium, nonstick skillet over medium-low heat until melted and bubbling slightly. Add the brown sugar, honey, cumin, salt, and cayenne and cook, stirring constantly with a wooden spoon, for about 1 minute. Add the walnuts and stir to coat the nuts evenly with the butter mixture. Continue cooking, stirring constantly, until the nuts are glazed and toasted, about 10 minutes. Do not let the nuts burn. Remove the skillet from the heat and allow the nuts to cool completely. Drain the nuts on paper towels if they appear greasy, and break them into smaller pieces with your fingers, if desired. Set aside.

CONT'D

3 firm, slightly underripe pears such as Comice, Anjou, or Bartlett

2 tablespoons water

1 tablespoon unsalted butter, cut into 6 small pieces

Freshly squeezed juice of 1 lemon

For the Spicy Honey-Glazed Walnuts:

3 tablespoons (1½ ounces) unsalted butter

¼ cup (2 ounces) firmly packed dark brown sugar

1 tablespoon good-quality honey

½ teaspoon ground cumin

½ teaspoon salt

⅛ teaspoon cayenne pepper

1½ cups (6 ounces) walnut halves

For the vinaigrette:

2 teaspoons Dijon mustard

1½ tablespoons balsamic vinegar

⅓ cup (2.7 ounces) extra-virgin olive oil

Freshly squeezed juice of ½ lemon

Salt and freshly ground black pepper

2 heads Boston or other mild lettuce, leaves separated, washed, and very well dried

4 ounces smoked Cheddar or smoked Gouda cheese, cubed

To make the vinaigrette, in a small bowl, combine the mustard and balsamic vinegar and stir lightly with a small wire whisk. Slowly drizzle in the olive oil, whisking constantly to create an emulsion. Whisk in the lemon juice. Season the dressing to taste with salt and freshly ground black pepper.

To compose the salad, carefully tear the lettuce into large pieces and place it in a large serving bowl. Slice each pear half lengthwise into 4 equal pieces and arrange the pears decoratively on top of the lettuce. Top the salad with the cubed cheese and some glazed nuts (see note). Drizzle a small amount of dressing over the salad; pass the remainder at the table.

NOTE: You will likely have some nuts left over, but they will remain fresh for several weeks if stored in an airtight container and refrigerated.

indian-spiced braised lamb shanks

***

SERVES 8

1 medium onion, peeled and coarsely chopped

6 cloves garlic, peeled

2 teaspoons *garam masala* (recipe follows)

1 tablespoon coarse salt

1 teaspoon freshly ground black pepper

½ cup (4 ounces) plain whole-milk yogurt

8 lamb shanks

1 cup (5 ounces) unbleached all-purpose flour

3 tablespoons vegetable oil, or more if necessary

2 cups (16 ounces) beef or lamb stock or broth (see note)

1 cup (8 ounces) dry red wine

2 large onions, peeled and cut into 1-inch slices

1½ pounds peeled and seeded butternut squash flesh, cut into 1½-inch cubes

1 pound parsnips, peeled and cut into 1-inch slices

Cooked white jasmine rice for serving

The first chef under whom I worked taught me the concept of a wet spice rub. I find it an easier and tastier way than brining to season meat before cooking. *Garam masala,* one of the ingredients in the rub, is traditionally a combination of, among other things, ground dried coriander seed, chili powder or ground dried chiles, cumin, black pepper, nutmeg, ginger, dried mango, fennel seed, mace, cloves, star anise, cinnamon, and cardamom. It's available in Indian groceries and specialty-food stores. I've included a recipe here for making your own simple version. If you like, you can substitute an equal amount of curry powder for the *garam masala.*

It is usually necessary to order lamb shanks ahead, since not all butchers or grocery stores keep them on hand. Ask to have the ball joints trimmed off the ends.

As a time-saver, most grocery stores sell plastic bags of peeled and seeded pre-cut butternut squash in the produce section.

Put the chopped onion and garlic in a food processor and pulse until coarsely chopped. Add the *garam masala,* salt, pepper, and yogurt and pulse to combine into a thick paste, or wet rub. Pat the mixture over the surface of the lamb shanks and refrigerate them, in a covered container, for at least 1 hour and up to 24 hours.

When ready to bake the lamb shanks, preheat the oven to 325°F with the rack in the lower third (but not the very bottom position) of the oven. Select a large, shallow, ovenproof casserole or roasting pan large enough to hold the shanks in no more than two layers. (You can also use a heavy-duty disposable aluminum roasting pan to cook the lamb. In this case, place the disposable pan on a sturdy baking sheet for support.)

CONT'D

Put the flour in a large bowl and dredge the shanks in the flour, one at a time, to coat all the surfaces with flour. Heat 3 tablespoons of the oil in a large, heavy skillet set over medium-high heat. When the oil is hot, add the lamb shanks, 3 or 4 at a time (in order not to crowd the pan), and cook, turning halfway through the cooking time, until the surfaces are browned, about 6 minutes on each side. Put the browned shanks in the casserole and brown the remaining shanks, adding oil if necessary. Add them to the casserole.

Deglaze the skillet by pouring in the stock and cooking over high heat for 1 or 2 minutes while you scrape down the sides of the skillet to incorporate the browned bits. Pour this liquid over the lamb shanks, add the wine, then scatter the onion slices, butternut squash, and parsnips over the shanks. Cover loosely with aluminum foil. Roast the lamb for 3 hours or until the shanks are very tender when pierced with the tip of a sharp knife. Remove the foil and roast an additional 30 minutes to brown the meat well.

To serve, spoon a portion of rice on each of 8 dinner plates, then place a shank on each portion of rice. Spoon some vegetables and cooking liquid over the meat and serve hot.

NOTE: Very high-quality meat, poultry, vegetable, and fish concentrates that can be reconstituted into world-class stocks are made by a company called More Than Gourmet. The concentrates can be found in most gourmet and specialty-food stores, by calling 800-860-9385, or by visiting www.morethangourmet.com.

garam masala

Place the cumin seeds, coriander seeds, cardamom seeds, pepper-corns, cinnamon sticks, cloves, fennel seeds, ginger, nutmeg, and star anise pods in a large, heavy skillet set over medium heat. Cook, shaking the pan to stir the spices, for about 5 minutes, or until the spices are hot and have begun to brown. Let cool completely, then grind to a fine powder using a spice grinder, food processor, or mortar and pestle. Store the *garam masala* in an airtight container in a cool, dry place for up to 2 months.

3 tablespoons whole cumin seeds

3 tablespoons whole coriander seeds

1 tablespoon whole cardamom seeds

1 tablespoon black peppercorns

2 cinnamon sticks, broken into small pieces

2 teaspoons whole cloves

1 teaspoon fennel seeds

1 teaspoon ground ginger

1 teaspoon ground nutmeg

2 star anise pods

chocolate meringue tart

***

SERVES 8

4 extra-large egg whites

¼ teaspoon cream of tartar

⅔ cup (5 ounces) granulated sugar

2 tablespoons natural
(not Dutch-process) unsweetened
cocoa powder, sifted

1 cup (8 ounces) heavy cream,
well chilled

2 tablespoons confectioners'
sugar, sifted

1 tablespoon white crème de
cacao liqueur

Chocolate curls or shaved chocolate
for garnish (see notes)

**Light as a cloud and easy on the eye,
this is a show-stopping yet uncomplicated dessert that can be
made in two stages and assembled just before serving.**

Preheat the oven to 300°F with the rack in the center position.
Generously butter a 10-inch pie plate; dust with flour and knock out
the excess.

Put the egg whites and cream of tartar in the spotlessly clean bowl
of a stand mixer. (You may use a copper mixing bowl and a handheld
electric mixer; in this case, omit the cream of tartar.) Using spotlessly
clean beaters, beat the egg whites on low speed until foamy, then
increase the speed to medium and slowly add the granulated sugar,
beating until the meringue holds stiff, but not dry, peaks. Reduce the
speed to low and add the cocoa; mix only until combined. Pour and
scrape the batter into the prepared pie plate; use a rubber spatula to
smooth the top, building the rim slightly higher and thicker than the
center. Bake for 1 hour, or until the surface is no longer sticky. Turn
off the oven and leave the door closed; allow the meringue to cool
completely before removing it from the oven. The meringue can
remain at room temperature, uncovered, for several days.

Just before you plan to serve the tart, put the heavy cream in a chilled
bowl and, using chilled beaters, beat the cream on high speed until it
holds soft peaks. On low speed, mix in the confectioners' sugar and
then the crème de cacao. Scoop the cream onto the meringue and use
a rubber spatula to make swirls. Garnish with chocolate curls or
shaved chocolate. Cut into wedges and serve.

NOTE: To make chocolate curls, line a small tray with parchment or
waxed paper; set aside. Use a hair dryer to slightly soften the surface
of a thick block of dark chocolate—just heat it for a few seconds using
a waving motion—you don't want it to get too soft. Drag a vegetable
peeler or chef's knife held at an angle across the surface (this will take
some practice, but you can eat the outtakes) until curls form. Use a

metal spatula to remove the curls to the prepared tray and store at room temperature until ready to use.

NOTE: To make shaved chocolate, run the edge of a thick block of chocolate over the coarse holes of a metal grater onto a small tray lined with parchment or waxed paper, or directly onto the dessert.

New Hampshire

Name your sport—**New Hampshire**'s ready for you. Work up a lusty appetite skiing (downhill and cross-country), skating (hockey or figure), fishing (summer and winter), canoeing, kayaking, hiking, mountain climbing, or sailing, then come home to meals that will restore your energy and put you in great shape for the next day's activities.

"TWELVE QUICK TIPS" COURTESY OF
THE GREAT ROTARY FISHING DERBY BROCHURE:
"TEST THE ICE! BEWARE! WIND AND CURRENT BREAK ICE.
DRESS IN LAYERS. BRING FOOD AND HOT DRINKS.
FISH WITH A PARTNER. DON'T GATHER IN LARGE GROUPS.
NO FIRES ON THE ICE. BRING BLANKETS AND A FIRST-AID KIT.
IF YOU FALL IN, REACH FOR ICE, KICK AND
ROLL TO SAFETY. FOLLOW FISHING REGULATIONS.
DON'T DRIVE CARS ONTO ICE. CLEAN UP!"
AND, MAY I ADD, EAT A HEARTY BREAKFAST.

red flannel salmon hash
page No. 141

english muffin bread
page No. 142

fireball
page No. 144

poached prunes with cinnamon mascarpone
page No. 145

red flannel salmon hash

***

SERVES 6

**Here's a new take on an old classic.
I find this hash lighter in texture and a tad more elegant
(if, indeed, that word can be applied to hash)
than the old standard. It's a much prettier color as well.
If you boil the potatoes and cook and flake the fish
the night before, assembly the next morning is a matter of
browning the potatoes and then adding the cooked fish.
When prepared like this, the entire cooking time
is shortened to less than 30 minutes.
Top with fried or poached eggs, if you like.**

5 Idaho potatoes (about
1½ pounds), peeled and cut
into 1-inch cubes (4 cups cubes)

2 tablespoons mild olive oil

1 fresh salmon fillet (about 1 pound)

4 tablespoons (2 ounces)
unsalted butter

1 medium onion, peeled and
chopped into ½-inch pieces

½ teaspoon salt

2 ounces thick-cut smoked salmon,
cut into ½-inch cubes

1 teaspoon grated lemon zest

1 tablespoon capers

Put the potatoes in a large saucepan, cover with water, and bring the water to a boil over high heat. Reduce the heat to medium and allow the potatoes to simmer until they are tender, about 10 minutes. Drain the potatoes and allow them to cool in a colander.

Meanwhile, heat the olive oil in a large, nonstick skillet over medium-high heat. When the oil is shimmering, add the fresh salmon fillet, skin side down. Allow the fillet to cook undisturbed for 5 minutes, until the skin is browned. Carefully flip the salmon over and cook for another 5 minutes, or until the fish is cooked through. Transfer the fish to a platter and use a fork to remove the skin from the salmon; discard the skin. Use the fork to flake the fish, removing any bones you find. Set the fish aside on a plate.

When the potatoes are cool, melt the butter in the pan you used to cook the fish. Add the onion and cook over medium heat, stirring, for about 3 minutes, until golden. Add the potatoes and spread them in an even layer. Allow to cook undisturbed over medium heat for 10 minutes, until the potatoes are browned. Use a spatula to flip the potatoes and allow them to cook for another 10 minutes. Sprinkle with the salt. Add the flaked salmon and mix with the spatula until well incorporated. Cook for 3 minutes, until the fish is heated through. Add the smoked salmon pieces, lemon zest, and capers and cook, tossing, for another minute. Serve immediately.

english muffin bread

***

MAKES 1 LOAF

2 cups (10 ounces) unbleached all-purpose flour

½ cup (2.5 ounces) whole-wheat flour

1 tablespoon cornmeal

1½ teaspoons granulated sugar

1½ teaspoons active dry yeast

1 teaspoon salt

1¼ cups (10 ounces) buttermilk (see note), heated to 110°F (very warm to the touch)

⅛ teaspoon baking soda

This recipe, with a few changes, comes from James Beard's classic book *Beard on Bread* (Knopf, 1973). I view it as a mini-miracle, because reading the recipe you'll never believe it is going to work, and in fact you'll still be dubious as you put it in the microwave to "bake." You'll look at store-bought English muffins with a bit of disdain once you've toasted a piece of this unique bread.

Combine 1 cup of the all-purpose flour with the whole-wheat flour, cornmeal, sugar, yeast, and salt in a medium mixing bowl and whisk lightly until combined. Slowly add the warm buttermilk while stirring with a wooden spoon until smooth. Add the remaining 1 cup of all-purpose flour and continue beating by hand until the batter is stiff and just slightly sticky.

Scrape the dough into another oiled, medium bowl. Cover with plastic wrap and set in a warm, draft-free place until doubled in bulk, about 1 hour. With a wooden spoon, stir down the batter to release the gas and deflate the dough. Dissolve the baking soda in 1 tablespoon of warm water and add this solution to the batter. Use the wooden spoon to mix until distributed evenly. Butter a 6-cup microwave-safe loaf pan and put the batter in the pan. Cover it with plastic wrap and set aside again in a warm place until doubled in bulk, about 30 minutes.

Place the loaf pan in the microwave and cook the dough on full power (high) for 6½ minutes. The bread will still be doughy, full of holes, and raw-looking; this is fine. Cool the dough in the pan for 5 minutes, and then turn it out onto a wire rack. Let cool completely.

To serve, cut as many slices as desired and toast them until crisp and golden brown.

NOTE: Powdered buttermilk, found in the baking section of most supermarkets, eliminates the need to keep fresh buttermilk in the refrigerator. Simply add to your recipe with the dry ingredients the amount of powder specified on the package, then substitute water for the buttermilk called for in the recipe. Store the powdered buttermilk in the refrigerator for up to 1 year.

fireball

For the simple syrup:

1 cup (8 ounces) cold water

1 cup (8 ounces) granulated sugar

1 cinnamon stick

3 tablespoons (1½ ounces) brandy

1 teaspoon pure vanilla extract

3 ounces whole milk

3 ounces heavy cream

Ground cinnamon for garnish

**Affectionately known as the "Velvet Fist,"
this cocktail will light a gentle fire in the coldest of bellies
and help you to understand why many folks would
choose ice fishing over a Caribbean holiday.
The leftover simple syrup will keep, refrigerated
in a glass jar, for several weeks.**

To make the simple syrup, in a small saucepan, combine the water, sugar, and cinnamon stick. Bring to a vigorous simmer and cook, stirring occasionally, until the sugar is fully dissolved. Remove from the heat and set aside to cool to room temperature. Remove the cinnamon stick.

Fill a cocktail shaker halfway with ice cubes. Add the brandy, vanilla, 1 tablespoon of the simple syrup, the milk, and heavy cream. Cover and shake well. Strain into a chilled highball glass. Sprinkle with cinnamon and serve.

poached prunes with cinnamon mascarpone

***

**We're not supposed to call them prunes anymore.
They've been upgraded to "dried plums."
Whatever you call them, you will find this extremely
grown-up preparation irresistible as is,
on cereal or ice cream, or, without the mascarpone,
as a sweet condiment with game dishes.**

To prepare the prunes, put the prunes, cinnamon stick, quartered lemon, Marsala, and orange juice in a medium saucepan. Add just enough water to cover the fruit. Cover and bring to a gentle simmer. Cook until the prunes are very tender but not mushy, about 30 minutes. Allow the prunes to cool to room temperature in the covered pan. Remove the cinnamon stick and lemon and transfer the prunes and their liquid to a covered container. Refrigerate until ready to serve. (The prunes can be refrigerated, covered, for up to 2 months.)

To make the Cinnamon Mascarpone, whisk together the mascarpone, sugar, and cinnamon in a small bowl.

To serve, spoon prunes and their liquid into individual dishes and top with a generous dollop of the Cinnamon Mascarpone.

For the prunes:

24 ounces (about 4 cups) dried pitted prunes

1 cinnamon stick

1 lemon, quartered

1 cup (8 ounces) sweet Marsala wine or sweet vermouth

2 cups (16 ounces) orange juice

For the Cinnamon Mascarpone:

8 ounces mascarpone cheese

1 tablespoon granulated sugar

½ teaspoon ground cinnamon

THOSE WHO HAVE READ *A WALK IN THE WOODS,*
BILL BRYSON'S HYSTERICALLY FUNNY ACCOUNT OF WALKING
THE APPALACHIAN TRAIL FROM GEORGIA TO MAINE, WILL UNDERSTAND
WHY SOME PEOPLE CALL IT THE APPALACHIAN *TRIAL.*
BRYSON'S BOOK IS REQUIRED READING FOR ANYONE CONTEMPLATING
SUCH AN ADVENTURE. FOR MY MONEY,
A LOVELY AFTERNOON HIKE FORTIFIED WITH A TASTY PICNIC
IS ALL THE ADVENTURE I NEED FOR A SUMMER DAY.

lemon-limeade
page No. 147

roasted veggie roll-ups
page No. 148

gorp
page No. 149

fig-date bars
page No. 150

lemon-limeade

**If life hands you lemons (and limes),
you're all set to make this refreshing thirst-quencher.**

In a small saucepan, combine 1 cup of the cold water with the sugar and bring to a vigorous simmer, stirring occasionally until the sugar is fully dissolved. Remove the syrup from the heat and set aside.

In a 2-quart pitcher, combine the lemon and lime juices with ¾ cup of the syrup. (Store any leftover syrup in a glass jar in the refrigerator for up to several weeks; it's a terrific way to sweeten iced tea or iced coffee.) Add the remaining 4 cups of cold water and stir to combine. Taste, and add more of the syrup if you prefer a sweeter drink. Fill 8 tall glasses with ice and divide the lemon-limeade among the glasses. Serve immediately.

5 cups (40 ounces) cold water

1 cup (8 ounces) granulated sugar

Freshly squeezed juice of 5 lemons
(about 1 cup juice)

Freshly squeezed juice of 6 limes
(about ¾ cup juice)

roasted veggie roll-ups

***

For the roasted vegetables:

¼ cup (2 ounces) plus
2 tablespoons mild olive oil

1 yellow bell pepper, halved,
seeded, and cut into ½-inch strips

1 red bell pepper, halved, seeded,
and cut into ½-inch strips

1 large red onion, halved from root
to stem, peeled, and cut into
¼-inch slices

2 medium zucchini squash,
trimmed and cut on the diagonal
into ½-inch slices

2 medium yellow summer squash,
trimmed and cut on the diagonal
into ½-inch slices

1 teaspoon kosher or coarse salt

For the Garlic-Tofu Spread:

1 clove garlic, peeled

7 ounces soft tofu

1½ teaspoons balsamic vinegar

½ teaspoon salt

1 tablespoon mild olive oil

6 pieces soft flatbread such as
lavosh, or three pita loaves
separated into 6 pieces

12 leaves romaine lettuce, washed
and well dried

Kosher or sea salt and freshly
ground black pepper

**When you've hiked all morning and are
in dire need of nourishment, instant gratification is as
easy as unwrapping one of these convenient power-packed
lunches that can be eaten out of hand. The seasoned
tofu spread is a delicious complement for the filling,
but a time-saving substitute is Boursin cheese,
found in most supermarket dairy cases. If you are using
the Boursin, bring it to room temperature
before making the roll-ups.**

To roast the vegetables, preheat the oven to 400°F with the rack in the upper third (but not the highest position) of the oven. Oil a large, rimmed baking sheet with the 2 tablespoons olive oil. Place the yellow and red bell peppers, onion, zucchini, and summer squash on the baking sheet and drizzle with the remaining ¼ cup of olive oil. Sprinkle with the salt and bake, uncovered, for 45 minutes, until the vegetables are tender and beginning to brown. Stir and turn the vegetables over halfway through the baking time. Allow to cool on the baking sheet.

To make the garlic-tofu spread, place the garlic clove in the work bowl of a food processor and process until it is chopped. Add the tofu, vinegar, salt, and olive oil and process until the mixture is very smooth. Transfer the purée to a small mixing bowl. (To mix the spread by hand, mince the garlic and combine it with the tofu, vinegar, salt, and olive oil in a medium bowl. Mix well until very smooth.)

To assemble the sandwiches, place a piece of bread on a work surface and spread it with some of the garlic spread. Cover the surface with a thin layer of vegetables and 2 lettuce leaves. Sprinkle with salt and pepper to taste. Roll tightly from one of the long sides. Continue making sandwiches with the remaining ingredients. Wrap the sandwiches in plastic wrap or parchment paper until ready to eat. They will keep at room temperature for several hours, or longer if stored in an insulated carrier with an ice pack.

gorp

***

MAKES 3 ½ CUPS

GORP started out as the acronym for
"**Good Old Raisins and Peanuts,**" but quickly morphed
into a mixture of any nibbles that someone
thought went together, or found while cleaning out a pantry.
I, for one, like the sweet and salty yin and yang
going on in this mix, and I think the hikers
in your crowd will as well.

Mix the apricots, cranberries, cashews, almonds, peanuts, chocolate chips, and pumpkin seeds together in a large bowl and toss well. Store in an airtight container at room temperature for up to 4 days.

½ cup (2 ounces) dried apricots, snipped with scissors into ½-inch pieces

½ cup (2 ounces) dried cranberries

½ cup (2 ounces) roasted, salted cashews

½ cup (2 ounces) sliced almonds

½ cup (2 ounces) roasted, salted peanuts

½ cup (2.5 ounces) chocolate chips

½ cup (2 ounces) roasted, salted pumpkin seeds

fig-date bars

If you are a fan of Fig Newtons, you'll love this recipe. While not exactly the same, the fillings and crust are so similar (at least in my mind) that you'll think you're back in grade school sitting in front of an open lunch box, deciding to eat dessert first.

For the crust:

3 cups (15 ounces) unbleached all-purpose flour

1 teaspoon baking powder

½ teaspoon baking soda

½ teaspoon salt

½ cup (1 stick; 4 ounces) unsalted butter, at room temperature

½ cup (4 ounces) granulated sugar

½ cup (4 ounces) regular molasses (not blackstrap)

1 extra-large egg

For the filling:

8 ounces dates (1½ packed cups, about 30 dates), pitted

8 ounces dried figs (1½ packed cups, about 20 medium figs), tough stems removed

¾ cup (6 ounces) orange juice

Preheat the oven to 375°F with the rack in the center position. Lightly butter a 9-by-13-by-2-inch metal baking pan. Line it with a 9-by-20-inch piece of parchment paper positioned lengthwise in the pan so that the parchment extends beyond the length of the pan. Cut a 13-by-13-inch piece of parchment and lay it across the width of the pan; the piece should just line the bottom of the pan and up the long edges of the pan. Press all the parchment well against the sides of the pan. Butter the exposed parchment surface; set the pan aside.

To make the crust, put the flour, baking powder, baking soda, and salt in a medium bowl and whisk together. Set aside. Beat the butter with the sugar in the bowl of a stand mixer on high speed until the butter is light and fluffy. Add the molasses and egg; beat well. The mixture may look curdled, but that's okay. Scrape down the sides of the bowl and reduce the mixer speed to low; mix in the flour mixture. Mix just until the flour is incorporated.

Divide the dough in half and wrap one half well in plastic wrap; refrigerate it while you prepare the bottom crust and filling. Use your lightly floured fingers to press the other half of the dough evenly into the bottom of the prepared pan. Bake for 10 minutes, until the crust has browned a little and feels a little dry. Remove the pan from the oven and let it cool. Reduce the oven temperature to 350°F.

To make the filling, put the dates and figs in a medium saucepan. Add the orange juice and simmer the mixture, covered, until the fruit softens and the orange juice is almost absorbed, about 10 minutes. Allow the fruit to cool for 5 minutes, then scrape it into the bowl of a food processor fitted with the metal blade. Process until the fruit is roughly puréed with no large visible pieces of fruit remaining. Spread the fruit mixture evenly over the dough in the pan. Remove the second half of the dough from the refrigerator and roll it between two sheets of parchment paper into a rectangle roughly the size of the top of the pan. Remove the top piece of parchment and use the bottom piece of parchment to help flip the dough onto the fruit filling. Gently trim the dough to fit into the pan. Use dough scraps to patch any cracks in the dough.

Bake until the top has browned and feels firm to the touch, about 30 minutes. Transfer the baking pan to a wire rack and allow to cool for 10 minutes, then use the parchment paper extensions to lift the bar from the pan. Set it on a wire rack to cool completely before cutting into bars. Store the bars at room temperature in an airtight container for up to 3 weeks.

COMMUNITY BENEFITS LIKE THE TRADITIONAL
FIREHOUSE BARBECUE ALWAYS ATTRACT AN EAGER AND
HUNGRY ASSEMBLAGE OF TOWNIES AND TOURISTS.
AS SOON AS THE FIREMEN LIGHT UP THE GRILL AND THROW
ON THE BURGERS, AN APPRECIATIVE CROWD GATHERS.
GET IN LINE EARLY SO AS NOT TO MISS OUT ON
THIS TASTY INDEPENDENCE DAY TRADITION.

three-cabbage slaw
page N°. 153

sweet potato salad
page N°. 154

cheddar-stuffed burgers on roasted garlic bread
page N°. 158

barbara lauterbach's firehouse brownies
page N°. 160

three-cabbage slaw

***

SERVES 8

**There is an extravagant array
of cabbages to be found in most supermarkets.
For such a workaday vegetable, the choices can be dizzying.
The good news is that virtually any cabbage
you choose can be part of the namesake threesome
in this recipe. The more you can choose cabbages
of distinct colors, the more this will look like
a bowl of delightfully colored confetti.**

1 small head napa cabbage (about 1 pound), cored and shredded into ¼-inch slices (about 4 cups)

½ small head red cabbage (about 10 ounces), cored and shredded into ¼-inch slices (about 3 cups)

½ small head savoy cabbage (½ pound), cored and shredded into ¼-inch slices (about 3 cups)

1 large carrot, peeled and shredded

For the dressing:

½ teaspoon celery seed

½ teaspoon dry mustard

1 teaspoon salt

1 teaspoon fresh lemon juice

2 tablespoons orange juice

¼ cup (2 ounces) granulated sugar

¼ cup (2 ounces) apple cider vinegar

½ cup (4 ounces) mild olive oil

Place all the cabbage slices and the carrot shreds in a very large bowl. Set aside.

To make the dressing, place the celery seed, mustard, salt, lemon juice, orange juice, sugar, and vinegar in the work bowl of a food processor. Turn on the processor and add the olive oil very slowly while the machine is running. Continue to process until the dressing is thickened and all the oil is added. (To make the dressing by hand, put the celery seed, mustard, salt, lemon and orange juices, sugar, and vinegar in a medium mixing bowl and whisk together. Add the olive oil in a very thin, steady stream, whisking constantly until the mixture thickens and all the oil is added.)

Pour the dressing over the vegetables in the bowl and mix well. Refrigerate for at least 1 hour and up to 24 hours before serving, to allow the flavors to meld.

The dressing can be made a day in advance and refrigerated until ready to use. The slaw ingredients can be mixed together and refrigerated, with or without the dressing, up to 24 hours before serving.

sweet potato salad

4 sweet potatoes (8 to 10 ounces each), peeled and cut into ¾-inch cubes

1 cup (4½ ounces) hazelnuts, toasted and skinned (see note), then coarsely chopped

½ red onion, peeled and cut into ½-inch dice

2 teaspoons toasted mild sesame oil

1 tablespoon hazelnut oil (you may substitute walnut oil or vegetable oil)

2 teaspoons soy sauce

1½ teaspoons fresh mint leaves, minced

1 teaspoon salt

½ teaspoon freshly ground black pepper

The combination of toasted hazelnuts, sweet potatoes, and mint is not one that may be the first to leap to mind when you're thinking of ingredient pairings, but they are in fact a heavenly mélange of flavors and textures that are perfectly suited. You can substitute jewel yams or any other kind of bright orange tuber for the sweet potatoes.

Put the potatoes in a medium saucepan and add cold water to cover. Place the pan over medium-high heat and bring to a boil. Boil, uncovered, until the potatoes are fork-tender but not mushy, 5 to 7 minutes. Do not overcook the potatoes or they will fall apart in the salad. Drain the potatoes and allow them to cool slightly.

In a large serving bowl, combine the hazelnuts, onion, and potatoes. Add the sesame oil, hazelnut oil, and soy sauce. Stir to combine, allowing the potatoes to absorb the dressing. Add the mint, salt, and pepper; taste and adjust the seasoning. Serve immediately or refrigerate for up to 24 hours. This is best served at room temperature, so let it sit on the counter for a few minutes before serving if it's been in the refrigerator.

NOTE: Purchase hazelnuts with the skins already removed, if possible. To toast the nuts, preheat the oven to 375°F with the rack in the upper third of the oven. Put the hazelnuts on a heavy-duty, rimmed baking sheet. Bake for 15 minutes, then briskly shake the pan back and forth to rotate the nuts. Bake for another 10 minutes or so, until the nuts are light golden brown. If the hazelnuts have their skins on, empty the hot nuts onto one half of a clean kitchen towel. Fold the other half over to enclose the nuts and rub the towel vigorously with your hands to rub the skins off. You will probably not be able to remove all the skins.

SWEET POTATO SALAD
see page No. 154

CHEDDAR-STUFFED BURGERS ON ROASTED GARLIC BREAD

see page N°. 158

cheddar-stuffed burgers on roasted garlic bread

***

SERVES 8

4 pounds chopped sirloin

½ cup snipped fresh chives

1 teaspoon dried basil

1 teaspoon dried tarragon

1 teaspoon dried oregano

1 teaspoon mild chili powder

1 teaspoon salt

½ teaspoon freshly ground
black pepper

A few drops of Tabasco or other
hot-pepper sauce

1 pound (16 ounces) aged Cheddar
cheese, cut into 8 equal slices

Roasted Garlic Bread (recipe
follows) for serving

**Fire up the grill, put these burgers on to cook,
and stand back and watch the line of folks standing there with
empty plates quickly form. The cheese inside the
burgers keeps them moist and juicy and adds a zing of flavor.
Think of them as sort of an inside-out cheeseburger.**

Prepare a fire in a charcoal grill or preheat a gas grill or the broiler.

In a large mixing bowl, use a wooden spoon or your hands to mix
together the chopped sirloin, chives, basil, tarragon, oregano, chili
powder, salt, pepper, and Tabasco to taste. Shape the mixture into
8 thick patties. Make a pocket in the center of each patty and insert
a piece of cheese into each pocket. Reshape the patties so that the
cheese is covered.

Grill or broil for 5 to 7 minutes on each side for medium-rare, or until
the meat is cooked the way you like it.

Serve on slices of Roasted Garlic Bread.

roasted garlic bread

***

**This is "downtown" dining at its best,
although the application of homemade garlic-infused oil
takes it several steps above regular old garlic bread. It makes
the perfect platform for the Cheddar-Stuffed Burgers.**

2 heads garlic

½ cup (4 ounces) mild olive oil

2 tablespoons (1 ounce)
unsalted butter

1 teaspoon coarse salt

½ teaspoon freshly ground
black pepper

1 large loaf soft Italian bread

Preheat the oven to 325°F with the rack in the center position.

Turn each head of garlic on its side and cut off the top portion of the
papery skin with a sharp knife. The uppermost part of each clove
should be exposed. Place the garlic heads in a ramekin large enough
to hold them side by side. Add the olive oil and butter. Cover with
aluminum foil and roast for about 45 minutes, or until the garlic is
golden brown and is tender when pierced with a skewer or the tip
of a sharp knife. Carefully remove the foil and cool. When the garlic
is cool enough to handle, remove it from the ramekin and use your
fingers to squeeze the pulp into a small bowl. Add the oil and butter
in which it cooked and mash with a fork until smooth. Mix in the salt
and pepper.

Slice the bread lengthwise and place it on a work surface, cut sides
up. Spread the garlic mixture over one cut surface. Place the other
half loaf on top to make a big sandwich. Wrap the loaf securely in
aluminum foil.

When ready to bake the loaf, preheat the oven to 375°F with the rack
in the center position. Bake for 20 minutes, or until the bread is hot.
Loosen the foil and allow the bread to bake another 10 to 15 minutes,
until the crust is crisp and golden brown.

The loaf can be made ahead and refrigerated, wrapped in aluminum
foil, for up to 24 hours, or frozen for up to 3 months.

barbara lauterbach's firehouse brownies

***

MAKES 24 BROWNIES

For the brownies:

4 ounces unsweetened chocolate, coarsely chopped

1 cup (2 sticks; 8 ounces) unsalted butter, cut into several pieces

4 extra-large eggs

2 cups (16 ounces) granulated sugar

2 teaspoons pure vanilla extract

1 cup (5 ounces) unbleached all-purpose flour

½ teaspoon salt

For the frosting:

2 tablespoons (1 ounce) unsalted butter, softened

1¼ cups (5 ounces) confectioners' sugar, sifted

3 tablespoons light cream

For the chocolate drizzle:

2 ounces semisweet chocolate

2 tablespoons (1 ounce) unsalted butter

These brownies are named "Firehouse Brownies" because my friend, cookbook author Barbara Lauterbach, served fourteen pans of them as the dessert at the annual Center Harbor Fire Department spaghetti supper. As she tells the story, "My neighbor was then the fire chief of Center Harbor, and he helped me out on Christmas Eve when the pipes froze at my B-and-B, I had a full house, and it was my first Christmas in New Hampshire on my own. He spent hours in my 1772 basement crawl space, armed with a hair dryer, thawing the frozen pipes; the temperature was ten below! The following summer, at the time of the annual event, I felt I owed him one. Neighbors are like that in Center Harbor."

Preheat the oven to 325°F with the rack in the center position. Butter the interior of a 9-by-13-inch baking pan. Dust with flour and knock out the excess. Set aside.

To make the brownies, melt the chocolate with the butter in a metal bowl placed over, but not touching, a pan of simmering water, or in a microwave. Stir with a wooden spoon until smooth. Set aside. Put the eggs and sugar in a mixing bowl and whisk until foamy. With a wooden spoon, mix in the chocolate mixture, the vanilla, and then the flour and salt, mixing only until there are no longer any visible traces of flour.

Pour and scrape the mixture into the prepared pan. Bake for 35 minutes, or until the top is dry and shiny. Cool the brownies in their pan to room temperature before frosting and drizzling them.

To make the frosting, cream the butter and confectioners' sugar together with a wooden spoon until blended. Add the cream and stir until smooth. Spread over the cooled brownies.

To make the chocolate drizzle, melt the semisweet chocolate and butter in a metal bowl placed over, but not touching, a pan of simmering water, or in a microwave. Dip the ends of a wire whisk or the tines of a fork into the warm mixture, then wave it back and forth across the surface of the brownies to form a decorative pattern. Use a long, sharp knife to cut the brownies into 2-inch squares, and an offset spatula to transfer them to a serving plate or covered container for storage. The frosted and drizzled brownies will keep, covered, at room temperature for several days, or they can be frozen in an airtight container for up to 3 months.

Vermont

With the notable exception of mud season (late March through April), each month brings cause to celebrate the **Green Mountain State**. World-class skiing in the winter; the sap running and consequent maple sugar production in early spring; glorious, blue-skied, long hot summer days just made for mountain biking or a refreshing swim in **Lake Champlain**; then fall brings the spectacular foliage that lights up the countryside and attracts leaf peepers from all around the world.

THE ENORMOUS WOODPILE STACKED
NEXT TO THE SHACK WITH BILLOWING STEAM
POURING OUT OF THE CHIMNEY IS A DEAD GIVEAWAY
THAT SERIOUS WORK IS GOING ON INSIDE.
BOILING DOWN THE SAP TO MAKE THE LIQUID GOLD
THAT IS MAPLE SYRUP IS NONSTOP, EXHAUSTING WORK.
THOSE WHO APPRECIATE THE TASTE OF
REAL MAPLE SYRUP ON PANCAKES, FRENCH TOAST,
OR ON A FINGER WIPING UP ERRANT DRIPS ARE
THE BENEFICIARIES OF ALL THAT LABOR.

hot spiced maple–grand marnier tea

classic omelets

maple-pecan scones

grilled pineapple

hot spiced maple–grand marnier tea

***

SERVES 8 TO 10

Even tea purists will agree that adding the right ingredients to the mix can make for some fine sipping. If you wish, you can substitute amaretto, an almond-flavored liqueur, for the Grand Marnier.

Bring the water to a boil in a large, nonreactive pot set over high heat. Turn off the heat and add the tea bags, cinnamon stick, cloves, and lemon juice. Allow to steep for 15 minutes, or until the liquid is a rich amber color. If you like stronger tea, allow the tea bags to steep for another 15 minutes or so.

Use a slotted spoon to remove the tea bags, the cinnamon stick, and the cloves. Stir in the liqueur and maple syrup. Taste and adjust the liqueur and syrup, if desired. Serve hot in warmed mugs or glasses.

12 cups (3 quarts) water

6 Constant Comment (or other orange-spiced tea) tea bags

1 cinnamon stick

8 whole cloves, tied in cheesecloth

Freshly squeezed juice of 1 lemon

½ cup (4 ounces) Grand Marnier or other orange-flavored liqueur, or more to taste

½ cup (4 ounces) pure maple syrup, or more to taste

classic omelets

***

12 extra-large eggs

3 tablespoons water

Scant 1 tablespoon salt

1½ teaspoons freshly ground black pepper

1 tablespoon chopped fresh herbs of your choice (optional)

2 to 3 tablespoons unsalted butter

Fillings of your choice (see note)

With omelets, as with most things that require speed and agility and coordination, the more you practice, the better you'll be. Keys to success are having all the ingredients prepared, at hand, and at room temperature; having a good nonstick, slope-sided pan; and possessing the ability to do several things at once. Start slowly, nailing down the technique for making one omelet, and then over time you'll find operating two pans at once an attainable goal.

I find using three eggs per person makes a good-size breakfast (and an omelet that needs no filling). If you do want to add fillings, suggestions are given below. Warm the serving plates in a 250°F oven about 15 minutes before you plan to start cooking; it's a shame to serve a nice, warm omelet on a cold plate.

Cooking time per omelet start to finish shouldn't take more than 3 to 4 minutes. If it's taking longer, turn up the heat on the stove top.

In a large bowl, whisk together the eggs, water, salt and pepper, and herbs, if using.

Put a generous teaspoon of butter in a 9- or 10-inch slope-sided, non-stick skillet set over high heat. Melt the butter until it sizzles but does not brown. Use a 1-cup ladle or 1-cup measure not quite filled (you want about ¾ cup of egg mixture per omelet, but you can always break more eggs if you run out toward the end) and ladle or pour one portion of the mixture into the pan. Immediately swirl and tip the pan so the egg mixture covers the bottom. Return to the heat and jerk the pan back and forth vigorously to keep the mixture moving, then use a fork to gently stir, taking care not to scratch the surface of the pan. You just want to stir for a few seconds to keep the omelet fluffy—not long enough to make scrambled eggs. With a fork or heat-proof rubber spatula, lift the edges of the omelet and allow any uncooked egg to run underneath. If the omelet is to be unfilled, simply flip one half over the other. If you are filling the omelet, place the filling on one half of the egg surface; use a wide spatula (or the action of the pan) to slip the uncovered side over the filling. Slide the omelet onto a warmed plate.

Continue to make omelets with the remaining egg mixture, adding butter for each new omelet.

At some point when you feel confident about making omelets, you can have two pans going at once—all it takes is practice.

NOTE: You can put anything you want in the middle of an omelet. Ingredients should be at room temperature (or warm in cases such as sautéed vegetables). Some of the most compatible things are grated Swiss or Cheddar cheese, mascarpone cheese or crumbled feta cheese, sliced ham, crisp-cooked crumbled bacon, thinly sliced or cubed smoked turkey, diced smoked salmon, sautéed onions and peppers, sautéed mushrooms, or cooked asparagus spears, to name a few.

maple-pecan scones

***

MAKES 10 SCONES

For the scones:

2½ cups (12.5 ounces) unbleached all-purpose flour

1 tablespoon baking powder

¾ teaspoon salt

1 tablespoon Lora Brody's Dough Relaxer (optional, for lighter fluffier scones with a longer shelf life; see notes)

¾ cup (3 ounces) pecans, toasted (see notes) and broken into pieces

1 tablespoon unsalted butter, melted

⅓ cup (2.67 ounces) grade B pure maple syrup (see notes)

1⅓ cups (10.67 ounces) heavy cream

For the glaze:

2 tablespoons (1 ounce) unsalted butter

1 cup (4 ounces) confectioners' sugar

2 tablespoons grade B pure maple syrup

Why anyone in his or her right mind would be willing to spend good money on a mediocre store-bought scone when you can make them yourself in hardly any time at all is beyond this penny-pinching New Englander.

Here is a recipe that celebrates Vermont's other finest commodity, pure maple syrup (the first is cheese). I can't stress how vital it is to use the real thing when you make these scones, and if you can find grade B—the real dark stuff— you'll be transported to scone heaven.

To make the scones, preheat the oven to 425°F with the rack in the center position. Line a baking sheet with a silicone pan liner, parchment paper, or aluminum foil. Set aside.

Combine the flour, baking powder, salt, and dough relaxer (if using) in a large mixing bowl and stir with a fork. Add the pecan pieces and toss to coat. In a medium mixing bowl, whisk together the butter, maple syrup, and cream. Dribble the maple syrup mixture over the dry ingredients. Mix well with a fork until it forms a crumbly mass. Turn the dough out onto a lightly floured surface.

Gently knead the dough by pushing it away from you ten times, turning the dough 90 degrees after each kneading motion, until the dough becomes smooth. Add a little flour to the work surface and your hands as you work, as necessary.

Flatten the ball of dough into a circle approximately 8 inches in diameter and ¾ inch thick. With a dough scraper or a sharp knife, cut the circle in half. Cut each half-circle into 5 equal wedges. Place the wedges at least 1 inch apart on the prepared baking sheet. Bake the scones for 14 to 16 minutes, or until the tops and bottoms are golden brown.

While the scones are baking, begin making the glaze: Melt the butter in a small saucepan over low heat. Whisk in the confectioners' sugar and the maple syrup. Continue whisking until the mixture is smooth. Remove the glaze from the heat.

When the scones are finished baking, remove the pan from oven. Carefully remove the scones from the baking sheet and place them on a wire rack set over a large piece of aluminum foil. Reheat the glaze if necessary, then pour it over the warm scones, smoothing the top of each scone with a knife and allowing the glaze to drip decoratively down the sides. Use a knife to lift the excess glaze from the foil and put it back in the saucepan to reuse as you continue to apply glaze to the scones. Serve warm.

The scones can be stored, tightly covered, at room temperature, but should be eaten within 24 hours. They can also be frozen in individual zippered plastic bags for up to 3 months. That way, you can remove a scone from the freezer the night before, and let it defrost on the kitchen counter to be eaten the next morning.

NOTE: Lora Brody's Dough Relaxer is available at www.lorabrody.com, 888-9-Bakeit; or at the King Arthur Flour Baker's Catalogue, www.kingarthurflour.com, 800-827-6836.

NOTE: To toast pecans, preheat the oven to 350°F with the rack in the center position. Place the nuts on a heavy-duty, rimmed baking sheet in a single layer and bake, stirring occasionally, until they are golden brown and fragrant, 10 to 12 minutes.

NOTE: Grade B maple syrup has been boiled longer than the light and less flavorful (although still wonderful) grade A. The evaporation process leaves a darker, thicker syrup with a more assertive maple taste.

grilled pineapple

***

SERVES 8

1 fresh ripe pineapple

4 tablespoons (½ stick; 2 ounces) unsalted butter, melted

1 cup (8 ounces) firmly packed dark brown sugar

¼ teaspoon ground cloves

¼ teaspoon ground ginger

¼ teaspoon ground nutmeg

If you've ever had a fresh Hawaiian pineapple, you've tasted nirvana and won't ever look back. So, the next time relatives or friends are going off to do the "aloha thing," tell them to forget the T-shirt and go for the fruit. Follow the instructions below for trimming a fresh, whole pineapple, or buy fresh pineapple rings, if available.

Preheat the broiler with the rack in the upper third of the oven. Line a rimmed baking sheet with aluminum foil or a silicone pan liner.

Twist the top off the pineapple and use a sharp, serrated knife to cut a thin slice off the bottom so it stands up without wobbling. Use a sharp knife to cut the outer peel from the pineapple and the tip of the knife to remove the "eyes." Slice the pineapple in half lengthwise and cut out and discard the core. Cut each half crosswise into 1-inch-thick half-rings. Arrange the half-rings close together in a single layer on the prepared baking sheet. Set aside.

Use a fork to mash the butter into the brown sugar. Mix in the cloves, ginger, and nutmeg; sprinkle the mixture over the pineapple. Watching carefully to prevent burning, broil for 2 to 3 minutes, or until the sugar is bubbling and has started to turn darker brown in places (it won't cook uniformly). Remove the baking sheet from the oven. Let cool for 5 minutes before serving.

I HAVE BEEN TOLD THAT MILE FOR MILE,
CROSS-COUNTRY SKIING BURNS MORE CALORIES
THAN ANY OTHER OUTDOOR ACTIVITY.
HERE'S A LUNCH MENU THAT WILL MAKE EVERY PULL
AND GLIDE WORTH THE EFFORT.

classic hot chocolate
page No. 172

split pea soup
page No. 173

smoked turkey sandwiches on cranberry-pecan quick bread
page No. 175

maple seven-layer bars
page No. 177

classic hot chocolate

1 cup (8 ounces) heavy cream

1 pound (16 ounces) semisweet chocolate, coarsely chopped

3 cups (24 ounces) whole milk

Marshmallows or whipped cream for garnish

No one would ever mistake this for your run-of-the-mill cocoa. For those of you looking for a serious chocolate fix, you've come to the right place. I like to use very bittersweet chocolate in this recipe, but you may prefer a sweeter drink, in which case use a slightly sweeter chocolate— imagine the fun you can have testing chocolate in order to make that decision.

Heat the heavy cream in a medium saucepan set over medium heat until tiny bubbles form around the edges of the pan. Remove the pan from the heat and add the chocolate. Stir until the chocolate melts. Divide this mixture among 6 mugs. Heat the milk in the same saucepan until small bubbles appear around the edges, but before a skin starts to form on top. Divide the milk among the mugs. Stir the hot chocolate in the mugs and serve immediately with marshmallows or a generous dollop of whipped cream.

split pea soup

**A meal-in-a-bowl is how you might want to
think of this stick-to-your-ribs, chase-the-cold-away soup.
It gets better with each reheating, so be sure to plan for leftovers.
You can leave out the meat and use vegetable broth if you
are feeding non-meat eaters. If you are feeding meat eaters,
try to find a kosher butcher who carries flanken, which
are a close cousin to short ribs. Of course short ribs, a ham bone,
a slab of bacon, or even cooked spare ribs will do nicely as well.**

3 pounds flanken (see recipe introduction) or short ribs, 2 racks of cooked spare ribs, a ham bone, or 1 pound slab bacon cut into 1-inch cubes

Flour for dredging

2 tablespoons mild olive oil

1 large onion, peeled and diced

3 cloves garlic, peeled and minced

12 cups (3 quarts) beef, chicken, or vegetable broth

4 large carrots, peeled and cut into ½-inch rounds

2 cups (16 ounces) dried split peas, rinsed and picked over for stones or dirt

2 teaspoons dried thyme, or the leaves of 6 sprigs fresh thyme

1 teaspoon dried sage, or 4 fresh sage leaves, minced

Salt and freshly ground black pepper

If you are using flanken or short ribs, place the flour in a shallow dish and dredge the meat to cover all the surfaces. If you are using a ham bone, spare ribs, or slab bacon, do not dredge them. Heat the olive oil in a large, heavy-bottomed pot or large pressure cooker. When the oil is hot, add the flanken, short ribs, spare ribs, or the ham bone and sear on all sides until nicely browned. If you're using bacon, cook it until crisp and well browned, without using any oil. Remove the meat, ham bone, or bacon and reserve. Add the onion to the pot and cook, stirring frequently, until the onion is translucent. Add the garlic and cook for 3 to 4 minutes, stirring frequently so the garlic doesn't burn.

Add the broth and use a wooden spoon to scrape the bottom of the pot, to dislodge any cooked bits from the meat and onions. Add the carrots, split peas, thyme, sage, and, lastly, whichever meat you have used. Cover and cook over medium-low heat, stirring every 15 minutes or so, until the soup is thick and the meat is very tender, about 2 hours. (If you are using a pressure cooker, cook on medium-high pressure for 50 minutes, then allow the pressure to release naturally; do not run cold water on the top of the pressure cooker.)

Using tongs or a slotted spoon, remove the meat. When cool enough to handle, remove the meat from any bones, chop it coarsely, and return it to the pot. Season the soup with salt and pepper to taste and serve hot.

This soup can be made ahead and refrigerated in a covered container for up to 4 days, or frozen for up to 6 months.

smoked turkey sandwiches
on cranberry-pecan quick bread

***

SERVES 6

To save time, you can buy a loaf of cranberry or other fruit quick bread in your local bakery. (Other breads complement these sandwiches, as well— the Irish Soda Bread on page 180 is a delicious option.) Consider spreading the bread with the Cranberry and Pear Chutney on page 55 for extra richness.

3 tablespoons whole-grain mustard

12 slices Cranberry-Pecan Quick Bread (page 176) or other fruit quick bread

18 to 20 ounces smoked turkey breast, thickly sliced

6 slices sharp Cheddar cheese

6 lettuce leaves, preferably bibb or Boston, washed and well dried

Spread a thin coating of mustard on each slice of bread. Top each of 6 slices with several slices of turkey, a slice of cheese, and a lettuce leaf. Top with the remaining 6 slices of bread to make sandwiches.

If the sandwiches are not served immediately, wrap tightly in plastic wrap and refrigerate for up to 6 hours.

CONT'D

cranberry-pecan quick bread

***

2 cups (10 ounces) unbleached all-purpose flour

1½ teaspoons baking powder

½ teaspoon baking soda

¼ teaspoon salt

¼ teaspoon ground cloves

¼ teaspoon ground cardamom

6 tablespoons (¾ stick; 3 ounces) unsalted butter, melted

⅔ cup (6 ounces) buttermilk (see note)

Finely grated zest and juice of 1 large navel orange

1 extra-large egg

⅔ cup (5.34 ounces) granulated sugar

1 cup (4 ounces) fresh or frozen whole cranberries, coarsely chopped

¾ cup (3 ounces) pecans, toasted (see note) and coarsely chopped

Preheat the oven to 350°F with the rack in the center position. Butter an 8½-by-4-by-2½-inch loaf pan. Dust with flour and shake the pan to coat the inside. Knock out the excess. Set aside.

Sift the flour, baking powder, baking soda, salt, cloves, and cardamom into a medium mixing bowl. Set aside. Combine the melted butter, buttermilk, and orange zest and juice in a small bowl. Set aside.

Use a whisk or a handheld or stand mixer on high speed to beat together the egg and sugar in a large mixing bowl until they are thick and light yellow in color. Whisk in or beat in on low speed the melted butter mixture. Scrape down the sides of the bowl with a rubber spatula several times during the mixing. Stir or mix in the flour mixture and finally the cranberries and nuts just to combine. Pour and scrape the batter into the prepared pan, and smooth the top with the rubber spatula.

Bake until a cake tester inserted in the center of the loaf comes out clean, 55 to 60 minutes. Transfer the pan to a wire rack and let the bread cool in the pan for 15 minutes, then turn the loaf out onto the rack. Set it right side up to cool completely before slicing.

The baked and cooled loaf can be stored at room temperature, wrapped in plastic wrap, for up to 2 days, or refrigerated for up to 1 week. It may also be frozen for up to 3 months.

NOTE: Powdered buttermilk, found in the baking section of most supermarkets, eliminates the need to keep fresh buttermilk in the refrigerator. Simply add to your recipe with the dry ingredients the amount of powder specified on the package, then substitute water for the buttermilk called for in the recipe. Store the powdered buttermilk in the refrigerator for up to 1 year.

NOTE: To toast pecans, preheat the oven to 350°F with the rack in the center position. Place the nuts on a heavy-duty, rimmed baking sheet in a single layer and bake, stirring occasionally, until they are golden brown and fragrant, 10 to 12 minutes.

maple seven-layer bars

***

MAKES 16 BARS

If you have a sweet tooth that's a challenge to satisfy, you have come to the right place. A tender maple-oatmeal crust cradles an assortment of goodies that melt together during baking to create a confection that is as pretty to look at as it is delicious to taste. Cut these into small bars— a little goes a long way.

Preheat the oven to 350°F with the rack in the center position. Butter a 9-inch square baking pan with 2-inch sides. Set aside.

In a small bowl, combine the oats, flour, maple sugar, and baking powder. Add the melted butter and mix well. Press the mixture into the prepared baking pan and bake until just golden, 10 to 12 minutes. Remove the crust from the oven and leave the oven on. While the crust is hot, scatter the butterscotch chips evenly over it, followed by the walnuts, chocolate chips, and coconut. Pour the sweetened condensed milk evenly over all. Scatter the maple sugar candy pieces over the top. Bake until bubbling and golden on top, about 20 minutes. Allow to cool, then cut into 16 squares with a small, sharp knife.

Store the bars at room temperature in an airtight container for up to 1 week.

1 cup (2.5 ounces) quick-cooking oats (not instant)

¾ cup (3.75 ounces) unbleached all-purpose flour

1 tablespoon granulated maple sugar or light brown sugar

½ teaspoon baking powder

½ cup (1 stick; 4 ounces) unsalted butter, melted

1 cup (5.5 ounces) butterscotch chips

1 cup (4.75 ounces) chopped walnuts

1 cup (5 ounces) semisweet chocolate chips

¾ cup (3.25 ounces) sweetened shredded coconut

One 14-ounce can sweetened condensed milk

2 ounces maple sugar candy, broken or chopped into ¼-inch pieces

THE CHURCH BASEMENT, VESTRY, TOWN HALL, OR
LIBRARY IS LINED WITH LONG TABLES AND FOLDING CHAIRS.
THE BUFFET TABLE GROANS UNDER THE WEIGHT
OF FOIL-COVERED PYREX CASSEROLES
AND BASKETS OF HOMEMADE ROLLS, COOKIES, AND CAKES.
THOSE ASSEMBLED LINE UP RIGHT ON TIME,
LEST THE THREE-BEAN SALAD OR TUNA NOODLE CASSEROLE
RUN OUT BEFORE THEY GET TO IT.
WELCOME TO A VERMONT POTLUCK SUPPER—
COME HUNGRY AND ON TIME!

the best tuna noodle casserole
page NO. 179

irish soda bread
page NO. 180

three-bean salad
page NO. 184

pear and candied ginger clafouti
page NO. 185

the best tuna noodle casserole

**An oldie but (oh so) goodie. You'll find variations
of this ultimate comfort dish at every church supper—but move
fast, because it's always the one to disappear first
onto happy folks' plates and then into their appreciative mouths.
You can use either water- or oil-packed tuna in this recipe.
I find the oil-packed far more flavorful.**

For the crumb topping:

4 ounces (about 32 crackers)
Ritz crackers

2 tablespoons (1 ounce) unsalted
butter, melted

½ cup (1½ ounces) grated
Parmesan cheese

¾ pound dried pasta (use a small
shaped type such as mini penne or
small shells)

2 tablespoons mild olive oil

2 medium onions, chopped into
¼-inch dice

2 celery stalks, sliced ¼-inch thick

8 ounces fresh mushrooms, brushed
clean and sliced into ½-inch pieces

½ teaspoon dried thyme

½ teaspoon salt

1 cup (4½ ounces) frozen peas,
thawed

Two 6-ounce cans tuna, drained

4 tablespoons (½ stick; 2 ounces)
unsalted butter

½ cup (2.5 ounces) unbleached
all-purpose flour

1 cup (8 ounces) whole milk

1½ cups (12 ounces) canned
low-sodium chicken broth

To make the topping, place the crackers in a zippered plastic bag and crush them with a rolling pin, meat mallet, or hammer. (It's better to have the pieces slightly non-uniform.) Put the crumbs in a medium bowl and pour the melted butter over them. Stir until they are evenly moistened. Add the Parmesan cheese and mix well. Set the crumb mixture aside.

Preheat the oven to 400°F with the rack in the upper third (but not the highest position) of the oven. Butter a 9-by-13-inch baking pan.

Bring a large pot of salted water to a boil and cook the pasta until it is just tender. Drain the pasta and set it aside.

Heat the olive oil in a large skillet over medium-high heat. Add the onions, celery, and mushrooms and sauté, stirring occasionally, until the vegetables are softened and golden. Pour the vegetables into a very large bowl and add the thyme, salt, peas, and tuna. Mix well, breaking up any large pieces of tuna. Add the drained pasta and toss to mix well.

In the empty skillet (no need to clean it), melt the butter over medium-high heat. When it stops foaming, add the flour and whisk for 2 minutes to brown it. Whisk in the milk and chicken broth. Continue whisking until the mixture simmers and is smooth and thickened, about 3 minutes. Add the sauce to the vegetables, tuna, and pasta in the bowl and mix well. Pour the mixture into the prepared baking pan and sprinkle the crumbs evenly over the top.

Bake until the filling is bubbly and the topping is golden, 20 to 25 minutes. Serve immediately.

irish soda bread

***

4½ cups (22.5 ounces) unbleached all-purpose flour

1 teaspoon baking soda

2 teaspoons baking powder

2½ teaspoons salt

3 tablespoons granulated sugar

1½ cups (12 ounces) buttermilk (see note), at room temperature

4 tablespoons (½ stick; 2 ounces) unsalted butter, melted

Freshly grated zest of 1 large orange

⅔ cup (2.7 ounces) golden raisins

½ cup (2 ounces) walnuts, coarsely chopped

1 egg white beaten with 1 tablespoon water, for egg wash

½ teaspoon caraway seeds

Don't wait for St. Patrick's Day to make this classic quick bread that's great at any meal: toasted with butter and jam for breakfast; for sandwiches at lunch; or for dinner in a bread basket or to mop up gravy. If you're a bread novice, this is a good place to try your hand, as you get to knead it a bit—just like a yeast dough. Take care not to overknead it, as that will make the bread tough. As with the scones (page 168), you'll find that homemade is much better than store-bought.

Preheat the oven to 375°F with the rack in the center position.

Put the flour, baking soda, baking powder, salt, and sugar in the bowl of a stand mixer. Mix on low speed for 5 seconds, or just until combined. With the mixer on low speed, slowly add the buttermilk, melted butter, and orange zest. Mix on low speed until the dry ingredients are moistened. Add the raisins and walnuts and continue mixing just until a rough dough forms and the nuts and raisins are evenly distributed, about 1 minute.

Transfer the dough to a floured work surface and knead it gently a few times until it becomes a cohesive ball. Form it into a mound approximately 7 inches in diameter. With a sharp knife, cut a cross in the top that extends the length of the dough and goes about ¼ inch deep. Brush the top with the egg wash and sprinkle with the caraway seeds. Bake for 65 to 70 minutes, covering the top loosely with aluminum foil if it begins to brown too much, until the top is deep brown and an instant-read thermometer inserted in the center registers 200°F. Transfer to a wire rack to cool slightly before slicing.

The completely cooled loaf can be wrapped in aluminum foil and stored at room temperature for up to 3 days, or frozen for up to 3 months.

NOTE: Powdered buttermilk, found in the baking section of most supermarkets, eliminates the need to keep fresh buttermilk in the refrigerator. Simply add to your recipe with the dry ingredients the amount of powder specified on the package, then substitute water for the buttermilk called for in the recipe. Store the powdered buttermilk in the refrigerator for up to 1 year.

PEAR AND CANDIED GINGER CLAFOUTI
see page N°. 185

IRISH SODA BREAD
see page № 180

three-bean salad

1½ pounds (24 ounces) fresh
green beans, ends trimmed

1½ pounds (24 ounces) fresh
wax beans, ends trimmed

⅓ cup (2.7 ounces) extra-virgin
olive oil

2 tablespoons white wine vinegar

Freshly squeezed juice of ½ lemon

2 cloves garlic, peeled and minced

Salt and freshly ground
black pepper

Two 14.5-ounce cans chickpeas,
drained and rinsed

1 cup oil-cured black olives,
pitted and finely chopped

¼ cup green onions, white parts
only, minced

2 to 3 sprigs fresh oregano
(optional)

**This isn't any old ordinary three-bean salad where
cans of beans are opened, drained, and thrown into a bowl.
We start with fresh beans, then jazz it up with olives and fresh
herbs, raising this version of a classic dish well above
what you may be used to.**

Prepare an ice bath for the beans by filling a large bowl with several handfuls of ice cubes and covering them with cold water. Set aside.

Bring a large pot of salted water to a boil over high heat. Add the green beans and wax beans and cook at a rolling boil until tender but not mushy, 4 to 5 minutes. Drain, then immediately plunge the beans into the ice bath. Drain again and pat the beans dry with paper towels. Set aside.

In a medium bowl, whisk together the olive oil, vinegar, and lemon juice until the mixture emulsifies. Add the garlic and salt and pepper to taste, and whisk lightly to combine.

To assemble the salad, toss the green and wax beans in the bowl with the dressing to coat them evenly. Use a slotted spoon to remove them from the dressing and mound them in the center of a serving platter. Add the chickpeas to the bowl and toss them to coat. Using the slotted spoon, arrange the chickpeas in a ring surrounding the green and wax beans. Sprinkle the black olives evenly over the beans and scatter the green onions on top. If desired, drizzle additional dressing over the salad. For a dramatic presentation, garnish with fresh oregano sprigs, if desired, standing tall in the center of the platter.

pear and candied ginger clafouti

***

SERVES 8

A clafouti is a French tart that is sort of like a quiche without the crust. This version, given to me by a French-Canadian friend who moved to Vermont as a teenager, contains no flour (which makes it perfect for your friends with gluten intolerance). So, if you have crust-avoidance syndrome or are in a real hurry, think of this lovely, quick, and easy dessert, which can also be made with apples, peaches, or nectarines. As long as the fruit is ripe and flavorful, you'll have a hit.

Preheat the oven to 350°F with the rack in the center position. Generously butter the bottom and sides of a shallow 8-cup gratin dish or casserole. Toss the pear slices, cranberries, and candied ginger in the buttered baking dish. Set aside.

In a medium bowl, mix together the eggs, brown sugar, heavy cream, and lemon zest and juice. Pour the egg mixture over the pear mixture. Drizzle the maple syrup evenly over all. Bake until set, slightly puffed, and browned on top, 35 to 40 minutes. Serve hot.

4 large pears (about 2½ pounds), peeled, cored, and cut into thin slices

½ cup (2 ounces) dried cranberries

3 tablespoons (1.25 ounces) candied ginger, minced

4 extra-large eggs

⅓ cup (2.5 ounces) firmly packed dark brown sugar

1 cup (8 ounces) heavy cream

Finely grated zest and strained juice of 1 large lemon

¼ cup (2 ounces) pure maple syrup

Maine

Wild, sweet **blueberries** no bigger than a drop of summer rain. Lobsters the size of beach balls. Deep woods that have never seen a road. An inlet- and island-studded, rock-bound coast that is made for meandering. A moose grazing by the roadside. A chance to see the **Northern Lights**. **Maine** is all these things, and so much more.

THE CRY OF THE LOON ECHOES OVER THE LAKE,
TROUT AND SALMON RIPPLE THE
STILL WATER, AND THE SUN'S FIRST RAYS
CAST LONG SHADOWS OVER THE
TALL PINES. HERE IS A RANGELEY-INSPIRED
BREAKFAST THAT WORKS AS WELL ON
A CAMP STOVE AS IN A KITCHEN
WITH EVERY MODERN CONVENIENCE.

dried fruit compote
page N°. 189

buttermilk waffles with blueberry sauce and crème fraîche
page N°. 190

turkey sausage patties
page N°. 193

dried fruit compote

**Health-food and most grocery stores offer
a dazzling selection of dried fruit.
Sometimes it's hard to choose among the dozens of choices.
Here's your chance to try as many different kinds
as you wish and end up with a luscious compote that has many
uses. Packed in nice glass jars, it makes a lovely gift.**

2½ cups (about 8 ounces) mixed dried fruit such as apricots, apple rings, peaches, pears, figs, raisins, and prunes (a.k.a. "dried plums")

1 cup (4 ounces) dried pitted cherries

½ cup (2 ounces) dried cranberries

2 navel oranges, peeled and cut into 2-inch chunks

1¼ cups (10 ounces) sweet red wine

2 cups (16 ounces) apple cider or orange juice

1 cinnamon stick

Using a pair of kitchen scissors coated with nonstick vegetable spray, cut large dried fruit such as apple rings, peaches, and pears into 2-inch pieces. Put all the dried fruit, the oranges, wine, cider, and cinnamon stick in a 4-quart saucepan set over medium-low heat. Cover and bring to a gentle simmer, stirring occasionally, and cook until the fruit is tender but not mushy, about 30 minutes. Let cool to room temperature. Remove the cinnamon stick and spoon the compote into clean glass jars. Seal tightly and refrigerate until ready to use. The compote will keep for several months.

Serve warm or at room temperature as a fruit course; as a condiment with chicken, turkey, pork, ham, or vegetarian main courses; or spoon over pound cake or ice cream for an easy dessert.

buttermilk waffles with blueberry sauce and crème fraîche

***

MAKES 8 WAFFLES

1½ cups (7.5 ounces) unbleached all-purpose flour

⅓ cup (2.7 ounces) granulated sugar

2 teaspoons baking soda

½ teaspoon ground nutmeg

1 teaspoon salt

1¼ cups (10 ounces) buttermilk

1 extra-large egg

½ teaspoon pure vanilla extract

1 tablespoon unsalted butter, melted and slightly cooled

Blueberry Sauce (recipe follows) for serving

Crème Fraîche (recipe follows) for serving

Calling for buttermilk as an ingredient in a recipe used to mean in most cases that the cook had to run out to the store to buy some. Now that there is shelf-stable powdered buttermilk available in most grocery stores and almost every health- or natural-foods store, you can have buttermilk waffles or pancakes (see note) whenever the urge or demand arises. The tangy crème fraîche that tops these waffles must be made a day in advance, and buttermilk powder is not suitable for making this topping. Use prepared crème fraîche, found in the dairy section of most supermarkets, if you like.

Preheat a waffle iron according to the manufacturer's instructions.

In a large mixing bowl, whisk together the flour, sugar, baking soda, nutmeg, and salt with a fork. In a glass measuring cup, combine the buttermilk, egg, vanilla, and butter. Slowly add the buttermilk mixture to the flour mixture and whisk gently with a fork until the dry ingredients are just moistened. Do not overmix or the waffles will be tough.

Ladle the batter into the waffle iron. (Do not add too much batter at once or it will drip down the sides of the waffle iron.) Cook according to manufacturer's directions. Serve hot, with the Blueberry Sauce and crème fraîche.

NOTE: To use this batter for pancakes, add enough additional buttermilk so that the batter flows easily and has the consistency of heavy cream.

CONT'D

crème fraîche

1 cup (8 ounces) warm
(skin temperature) heavy cream

2 tablespoons buttermilk, whole-milk
yogurt, or sour cream

Put the heavy cream and buttermilk in a glass jar, shake well to
combine, and allow to sit for 24 hours in a warm (70°F) place until
thickened. Use immediately or store, refrigerated in a tightly sealed
container, for up to 1 month, depending on the expiration date
of the cream.

blueberry sauce

***

MAKES ABOUT 2½ CUPS

¼ cup (2 ounces) granulated sugar

2 tablespoons cornstarch

2 cups (11 ounces) fresh or frozen
blueberries

½ cup (4 ounces) orange juice

Finely grated zest and juice of
1 lemon

**If you can get a hold of the tiny Maine blueberries
(either fresh or frozen), you'll find they pack flavor
not found in their plumper cousins.**

Combine the sugar and cornstarch in a small bowl. Set aside.

In a small saucepan over medium heat, combine the berries and
orange juice. Cook, stirring constantly, until the berries release their
liquid. Remove from the heat and stir in the cornstarch mixture.
Return the pan to low heat and cook, stirring constantly, until the
mixture thickens slightly and is no longer cloudy, 3 to 4 minutes.
Stir in the lemon zest and juice.

The sauce should be served warm. It can be made up to 3 days ahead.
Store in a covered container in the refrigerator, and reheat in either
the microwave or in a small saucepan set over low heat.

turkey sausage patties

Sparkles of sweet apple accent these savory patties, making them the perfect accompaniment for waffles, pancakes, or eggs. Cook them until they are quite brown so they will be crisp when served. The patties can be formed the night before and stored between layers of plastic wrap in a tightly covered container in the refrigerator to be cooked just before serving, or they can be cooked the day before and reheated in a hot skillet or in the microwave.

4 tablespoons vegetable oil, plus more if necessary

1 small onion, peeled and diced

2 cloves garlic, peeled and minced

1 pound (16 ounces) ground turkey (dark meat, if possible)

⅓ cup (1 ounce) finely chopped dried apple

2 teaspoons dried herbes de Provence (see note)

½ teaspoon fennel seeds

2 teaspoons salt

½ teaspoon freshly ground black pepper

Put 1 tablespoon of the oil in a heavy skillet set over medium-high heat. When the oil is hot, add the onion and cook for five minutes, stirring frequently, until golden brown. Lower the heat to medium and add the garlic, continuing to stir. Cook for 2 to 3 minutes, until the garlic is translucent. Transfer the mixture to a small bowl and set aside.

Put the turkey, dried apple, herbes de Provence, fennel seeds, salt, pepper, the onion and garlic mixture, and 2 tablespoons of the oil in the work bowl of a food processor fitted with the metal blade. Process until finely ground and well combined. Remove the blade. With dampened hands, form the mixture into 8 flat patties, each 3½ to 4 inches in diameter (each patty will weigh about 2½ ounces).

In a medium skillet, heat the remaining 1 tablespoon oil over medium-high heat until hot. Add the patties to the skillet. Cook until very well browned on both sides, about 3 minutes per side, adding more oil if necessary to keep the meat from sticking. Serve hot.

NOTE: Herbes de Provence is a mixture of dried basil, marjoram, rosemary, sage, summer savory, and thyme leaves, plus dried lavender leaves and flowers and crushed fennel seed. It is available in the spice section of most supermarkets and in specialty-food stores.

A VISIT TO ACADIA, MAINE'S ONLY NATIONAL PARK,
ISN'T COMPLETE WITHOUT "TAKING" TEA AT
THE FAMOUS JORDAN POND HOUSE. A SEAT ON THE VERANDA OR INSIDE
BY A PICTURE WINDOW AFFORDS A SPECTACULAR VIEW
OF BOTH THE POND AND NORTH AND SOUTH BUBBLE MOUNTAINS.
WHEN THE BASKET OF CRISP, GOLDEN POPOVERS
APPEARS AT YOUR TABLE, DON'T WASTE TIME—SPLIT THEM OPEN
AND INHALE THE SWEET STEAM.
WITH OR WITHOUT THE ACCOMPANYING STRAWBERRY JAM,
THEY ARE WHAT SPECIAL MEMORIES ARE MADE OF.

cucumber sandwiches

**Some consider this classic a throwback to a different era,
when ladies wore hats and white gloves to tea.
Perhaps it's time to welcome these sandwiches back—
you'll find them just as delectable now as your great aunts found
them back then. Use the long, narrow, virtually seedless
English variety of cucumber here.**

One 1-pound loaf thinly sliced good-quality white sandwich bread such as Pepperidge Farm

2 English hothouse cucumbers

½ cup (1 stick; 4 ounces) very soft unsalted butter

Salt

½ cup good-quality mayonnaise

1 cup finely chopped fresh flat-leaf (Italian) parsley

Use a serrated knife to trim the crusts from the bread. Peel the cucumbers and slice them into paper-thin rounds. Spread each slice of bread with a thin coating of butter. Arrange a layer of cucumbers on half of the slices, sprinkle lightly with salt, and place the other slices, butter side down, on top. Cut each sandwich into 4 triangles. Spread a thin coating of mayonnaise around the edge of each triangle and dip each edge into the chopped parsley.

Place the sandwiches on a platter and serve immediately, or cover tightly with plastic wrap and refrigerate for up to 4 hours before serving.

For variety, you may wish to substitute a thin slice of smoked salmon or some watercress for the cucumber in some of the sandwiches.

popovers with strawberry jam

5 extra-large eggs

2½ cups (20 ounces) whole milk

2¼ cups (11.25 ounces) unbleached all-purpose flour

2 tablespoons (1 ounce) unsalted butter, melted

2 tablespoons granulated sugar

½ teaspoon salt

Butter for serving

Strawberry Jam (recipe follows) for serving

Sitting on the porch of the Jordan Pond House, eating hot popovers dripping with butter and jam and watching the sunset, is my idea of heaven on earth. If a trip to Acadia National Park isn't in your immediate future, you can still emulate the popover experience. There's a certain magic and element of surprise to making popovers, starting with a batter that doesn't look like it holds much promise at all. Turn on the oven light and watch as the oven's heat causes the air pockets to swell and push the popover up into a crown of golden brown. You'll witness a great show with a delicious conclusion. The keys to popover success are making sure they are cooked enough (to prevent the insides from being soggy) and enjoying them piping hot from the oven.

Preheat the oven to 450°F with a rack in the center position. Generously butter the cups of two 12-cup muffin tins or popover pans.

In a large bowl, whisk the eggs, then add the milk, flour, melted butter, sugar, and salt. Whisk until there are only a few small lumps of flour left (some small lumps are okay).

Pour the batter into the prepared muffin or popover cups, filling the cups two-thirds full. Add water to any unused cups to keep them from overheating and scorching.

Bake for 15 minutes, then turn the heat down to 375°F and bake for another 15 minutes. Do not open the oven to peek at the popovers until the last 5 minutes of baking! When the popovers are tall and golden brown, remove from the oven. Gently poke the popovers with a fork or the tip of a sharp knife to allow steam to escape, then remove them from the tins and serve immediately with butter and the Strawberry Jam.

strawberry jam

You don't have to be into canning or preserving to make this jam,
since it's stored in the refrigerator after cooking.
The high sugar content will keep it from spoiling for up to
2 weeks as long as it is kept covered and cold.
The quality of the fruit is what is going to make your jam taste
as close as possible to fresh fruit, which good jam should
taste like (not sugar with flavoring). Seek out native-grown
strawberries, which are smaller and much more
flavorful than the water-filled giants available year round.

1 pound (16 ounces) fresh, small, sweet strawberries, hulled, rinsed, and patted dry

1 cup (8 ounces) granulated sugar

2 tablespoons lemon juice

Place a large handful of ice in a small metal bowl, add enough water
to cover, and place a metal spoon into the water to chill it.

Put the berries, sugar, and lemon juice in a large, heavy skillet set
over high heat. When the mixture starts to simmer, reduce the heat
to medium and cook, stirring continuously, until the mixture starts to
thicken. Skim and discard any foam that collects on the surface. After
5 minutes of steady cooking, quickly dip the cold spoon into the mixture and pull it out. If the jam is thick enough to coat the spoon and
the coating moves only slightly as you tilt the spoon, remove the pan
from the heat. If the jam is still runny, cook it for 2 minutes longer,
and then test it again with the cold spoon.

Remove the pan from the heat and, using a potato masher, very gently
crush the berries to make a lumpy mixture. Let cool, then spoon the
mixture into plastic or glass containers. Seal tightly and refrigerate
for up to 2 weeks, or freeze, in plastic containers only, for up to
6 months.

blueberry buckle

***

SERVES 8

For the topping:

4 tablespoons (½ stick; 2 ounces) unsalted butter, at room temperature

½ cup (4 ounces) granulated sugar

⅓ cup (1.7 ounces) unbleached all-purpose flour

½ teaspoon cinnamon

For the cake:

2 cups (10 ounces) unbleached all-purpose flour

2½ teaspoons baking powder

¾ teaspoon salt

¾ cup (6 ounces) granulated sugar

¾ cup (6 ounces) whole milk

4 tablespoons (½ stick; 2 ounces) unsalted butter, melted and slightly cooled

1 extra-large egg

1 pint (2 cups) tiny, wild blueberries

Buckle is a yellow cake mixed with fruit and topped with streusel crumbs before baking. This version comes from a woman who lived on a tiny island off Mt. Desert, Maine. Use the tiny, wild blueberries available in season in August, or use wild ones that have been frozen. You can make the buckle far in advance, as it freezes nicely, or serve it freshly baked, either warm or at room temperature. You could also make this without any fruit, in which case it would be a plain coffee cake.

Preheat the oven to 375°F with the rack in the center position. Butter an 8-inch square or 9-inch round cake pan.

To make the topping, put the butter, sugar, flour, and cinnamon in a small bowl. Stir with a fork to combine. Set aside while you make the cake.

To make the cake, put the flour, baking powder, salt, and sugar in a mixing bowl. Stir with a wooden spoon to combine. Put the milk in a 2-cup measure, then add the melted butter and egg. Stir with a fork just to combine, then add the milk mixture to the flour mixture. Mix gently to combine, then fold in the blueberries, stirring gently just to mix them in. Pour and scrape the batter into the prepared pan, and sprinkle with the prepared topping. Bake for 45 minutes to 1 hour, until the topping is well browned and a cake tester or toothpick inserted in the center of the cake comes out clean. Cool on a wire rack before cutting and serving.

jordan pond house oatmeal bars

***

MAKES 54 BARS

**What's tea without some sort of chocolate treat?
The combination of crunchy toasted oats crowned with a smooth
chocolate and peanut butter topping is irresistible.
Even if you can't eat these scrumptious nuggets while gazing over
the rocky outcroppings that ring the lawn of the
Jordan Pond House, they may inspire you to put that magical
site on your wish list of special places to visit.**

Preheat the oven to 350°F with the rack in the center position. Butter the sides and bottom of a 9-by-13-inch baking pan. Set aside.

Put the butter in the bowl of a stand mixer and beat on high speed until creamy. Add the brown sugar and beat on high until it is light and fluffy, about two minutes. Lower the mixer speed to medium and add the corn syrup and vanilla. Remove the bowl from the mixer and stir in the oats and peanuts with a wooden spoon. Spread the batter in the prepared pan and bake until the surface is dry and the edges have just begun to turn light brown, 15 to 17 minutes. Remove the pan from the oven and place on a wire rack to cool until lukewarm.

To make the glaze, melt the chocolate chips and peanut butter together in a small saucepan set over low heat. Stir continuously until the chocolate has melted and the mixture is smooth. Spread the glaze over the bars, smoothing the surface with an offset or rubber spatula. Let cool at room temperature or in the refrigerator, uncovered, until the chocolate has set, then cut into bars.

The bars can be stored in a covered container at room temperature for up to 1 week, or frozen for up to 3 months.

1 cup (2 sticks; 8 ounces) unsalted butter, at room temperature

1⅓ cups (10.67 ounces) firmly packed dark brown sugar

¾ cup (6 ounces) light corn syrup

1 tablespoon pure vanilla extract

5⅓ cups (12 ounces) quick-cooking oats (not instant)

1 cup (4 ounces) dry-roasted peanuts, coarsely chopped

For the glaze:

1¾ cups (8.75 ounces) semisweet chocolate chips

1 cup (8 ounces) smooth peanut butter

BAR HARBOR LOBSTER DINNER

NO TRIP TO THE MAINE COAST IS COMPLETE
WITHOUT A MEAL IN WHICH LOBSTER PLAYS A STARRING ROLE.
SOME FOLKS ORDER WHOLE LAZY MAN'S LOBSTER
(IN WHICH THE MEAT IS REMOVED FROM THE SHELL FOR YOU)
WHEN THEY SEE IT ON THE MENU,
BUT AS FAR AS OUR FAMILY IS CONCERNED,
A CHUNKY LOBSTER STEW IS THE BEST WAY TO ENJOY
NEW ENGLAND'S MOST FAMOUS CRUSTACEAN.
THE PROMISE OF A SHORTCAKE DESSERT MAKES YOU THINK TWICE
BEFORE INDULGING IN SECONDS ON THE STEW.

kathy gunst's lobster stew

corn, edamame, and red pepper salad

bacon batter bread

strawberry-rhubarb shortcakes

kathy gunst's lobster stew

***

SERVES 6

**My friend Kathy Gunst, who lives in southern Maine,
is the author of eight terrific cookbooks and the resident chef for
the show *Here and Now* on WBUR, Boston's preeminent
public radio station. I first "met" Kathy while
I was driving down the highway listening to the show.
She was making a chowder that sounded so enticing that,
completely distracted by her description of the dish and the sounds
of pouring, sizzling, and stirring coming from my radio,
I practically drove off the road. When I needed a perfect lobster
dish that represented the state of Maine, I knew
exactly whom to call. Kathy describes it as a cross between a
chowder and a seafood pan roast, and advises that if you precook
the lobster, the stew can be made in about 15 minutes.**

1 teaspoon salt

Two 2-pound live lobsters

3 tablespoons (1½ ounces)
unsalted butter

1 large onion, peeled and minced

2 cups (16 ounces) whole milk

1 cup (8 ounces) heavy cream

1 cup (8 ounces) fish stock
(see note)

Dash of sweet Hungarian paprika

Salt and freshly ground
black pepper

Dash of Tabasco or other
hot-pepper sauce

Oyster crackers for serving

Select a deep pot large enough to hold the lobsters. Add 2 inches of
water to the pot and the 1 teaspoon salt. Bring the water to a boil,
add the lobsters, shell sides down, cover, and cook at a rapid simmer
for 18 minutes. Don't overcook the lobsters or the meat will be
tough—especially since it will be cooked again in the stew. Drain in
a colander, then place the cooked lobsters under cold running water
until cool enough to handle. Working over a bowl to catch any liquid
(Kathy calls this "lobster juice") from the shells, remove the meat
from the tail and claws. Cut the meat into 1-inch pieces and refrigerate along with any juice in the bowl.

Melt 1 tablespoon of the butter in a large saucepan. Add the onion
and sauté, stirring frequently, for about 5 minutes, or until wilted and
light golden brown. Add the milk, cream, and fish stock and bring to a
gentle simmer. Stir in the reserved lobster meat and juice and simmer
for 5 minutes just to heat it through. Stir in the paprika. Season with
salt, pepper, and Tabasco sauce to taste.

CONT'D

Immediately ladle into 6 warmed bowls and top each with 1 teaspoon of the remaining butter. Pass the oyster crackers at the table.

NOTE: Very high-quality fish and shellfish concentrates that can be reconstituted into world-class stocks are made by a company called More Than Gourmet. The concentrates can be found in most gourmet and specialty-food stores, by calling 800-860-9385, or by visiting www.morethangourmet.com. Frozen fish stock is sold in some grocery stores.

corn, edamame, and red pepper salad

***

SERVES 8 TO 10

One 16-ounce bag frozen
shelled edamame

4 cups (16 ounces) fresh or frozen
corn kernels (see notes)

1 small red onion, peeled and
cut into medium dice

1 large red bell pepper, cut into
medium dice

½ cup (4 ounces) plain yogurt

1 scant teaspoon mild, toasted
sesame oil

1 tablespoon soy sauce

7 or 8 dashes of Tabasco or
other hot-pepper sauce

Salt and freshly ground
black pepper

2 tablespoons sesame seeds,
toasted (see notes)

Like a shower of multicolored confetti,
this beautiful salad will catch the eye of everyone at the table.
The juxtaposition of flavors—sweet corn, an accent of
hot pepper, the tang of yogurt, and the hint of sesame oil—
combine to make this something that will become
an oft-requested recipe. Be sure to add just a tiny amount
of sesame oil, as too much will take over the salad and
you won't be able to taste the other flavors.

Now that Japanese food is so ubiquitous, most Americans
can at least recognize fresh soy beans (edamame)
and appreciate their lovely, earthy taste. Shelled, frozen
edamame are available in most supermarkets
with the other frozen vegetables.

Cook the edamame and frozen corn (if using) separately in two
3-quart saucepans of salted, boiling water according to package
directions. Drain the vegetables and rinse them under cold running
water to stop the cooking. (If using fresh corn, see note.)

In a medium serving bowl, combine the edamame, corn, red onion,
and bell pepper. Set the salad aside while you make the dressing.

In a small bowl, combine the yogurt, sesame oil, soy sauce, and
Tabasco. Whisk lightly until smooth. Pour the dressing over the salad
and stir the ingredients together with a wooden spoon. Season to
taste with salt and freshly ground pepper. Sprinkle the salad with the
toasted sesame seeds. Cover the bowl with plastic wrap and refrigerate until ready to serve.

This salad may be served cold or at room temperature and may be
prepared up to 1 day in advance.

NOTE: To use fresh corn, bring a large pot of salted water to a boil.
Shuck 4 ears of sweet corn, carefully removing any silk. Cut off the
stem end and 1 or 2 inches off the top. Place the corn in the water,

cover, and cook for 4 minutes, or just until tender. Using tongs, remove the corn from the water and immediately run under cold water to stop the cooking. When cool enough to handle, place an ear of corn, stem side down, on a work surface and use a sharp chef's knife to run down the sides, close to the cob, cutting off the whole kernels. Separate the kernels from each other if necessary. Repeat with the remaining ears of corn.

NOTE: To toast sesame seeds, line a rimmed baking sheet with paper towels. Put the sesame seeds in a large, dry, heavy skillet set over high heat. Shake the pan briskly back and forth to agitate the seeds, or stir constantly with a wooden spoon, until the seeds turn light golden brown. Transfer immediately to the prepared baking sheet to cool; the seeds will continue to cook briefly, so be careful not to overbrown.

bacon batter bread

MAKES 1 LARGE ROUND LOAF

**Beautiful to behold and spectacular to taste,
this bread rises like a crown and will become the talk of the
breakfast table. If you are looking for an easy entrée into bread
making, then this one-bowl wonder is the recipe for you.**

4 cups (20 ounces) unbleached all-purpose flour, plus an additional ½ cup if necessary

1 tablespoon active dry yeast

½ teaspoon dried thyme

2 teaspoons salt

⅔ cup (5.34 ounces) warm water

1 cup (8 ounces) plain whole-milk yogurt, at room temperature

6 tablespoons (¾ stick; 3 ounces) unsalted butter, melted and cooled to room temperature

2 extra-large eggs, at room temperature

3 tablespoons honey

3 slices (6 ounces) thick-cut bacon, cut into fine dice, cooked until crisp, and drained

4 oil-packed sun-dried tomatoes, well-drained on paper towels and finely chopped

1 extra-large egg yolk mixed with 1 tablespoon whole milk or cream to make an egg wash

Put the flour, yeast, thyme, and salt in the bowl of a stand mixer fitted with the paddle attachment. Mix on low speed for 5 seconds just to combine. Turn the mixer off.

In a medium bowl, combine the water, yogurt, butter, eggs, and honey and whisk to combine. With the mixer still turned off, add the yogurt mixture to the flour mixture in the mixer bowl. Mix on low speed until all the dry ingredients are moistened, and the flour is no longer visible, about 20 seconds. Add up to ½ cup of additional flour, if necessary, to make a very soft, moist dough which will resemble something between a batter and a dough. Beat for 2 to 3 minutes on medium speed, then scrape the dough into a large oiled bowl. Cover with plastic wrap that has been lightly sprayed with nonstick vegetable spray and let rise in a warm place until doubled in bulk.

With floured hands, gently deflate the dough and turn it out onto a lightly floured work surface. Knead in the bacon and sun-dried tomatoes. Transfer the dough to a buttered 2-quart round casserole. Cover again with plastic wrap and let rise for a second time until doubled in bulk.

When ready to bake the bread, preheat the oven to 375°F with the rack in the lower third of the oven. Brush the top of the bread with the egg wash. Bake for approximately 1 hour, or until an instant-read thermometer inserted in the center of the loaf registers 200°F. Check the bread after 45 minutes, and if the top appears to be browning too fast, cover loosely with a sheet of aluminum foil. Remove the bread from the casserole dish and cool for at least 20 minutes on a wire rack before cutting into wedges.

strawberry-rhubarb shortcakes

***

SERVES 10

For the sauce:

3 cups (12 ounces) sliced rhubarb stalks (½-inch slices)

4½ cups (3 pints; 24 ounces) strawberries, hulled and halved

½ cup granulated sugar

½ cup (4 ounces) fresh orange juice (from 1 orange)

For the biscuits:

3½ cups (17.5 ounces) unbleached all-purpose flour

1¼ teaspoons salt

1 tablespoon baking powder

½ teaspoon baking soda

¼ cup (2 ounces) granulated sugar

1 tablespoon Lora Brody's Dough Relaxer (optional, for even flakier, more tender biscuits; see notes)

⅓ cup (2 ounces) solid vegetable shortening

¾ cup (6 ounces) buttermilk (see notes)

¾ cup (6 ounces) heavy cream

1 tablespoon unsalted butter, melted

For the whipped cream:

2 cups (16 ounces) heavy cream, chilled

2 tablespoons superfine sugar

1 tablespoon pure vanilla extract

Fresh rhubarb appears in the market in early spring and is available all summer long. In this recipe, it's imperative for both flavor and texture to select the smaller, tender stalks as opposed to the long, woody ones. While you can bake the biscuits several hours ahead and keep them uncovered at room temperature, there is nothing quite like the ethereal taste of hot-from-the-oven biscuits napped with the slightly piquant sauce of fresh berries and rhubarb.

To make the sauce, place the rhubarb, 3 cups of the halved strawberries, the sugar, and the orange juice in a medium saucepan. Bring to a simmer and cook over medium-low heat for 10 to 15 minutes, stirring occasionally, until the rhubarb is broken down and the sugar is dissolved. Remove from the heat, stir in the remaining 1½ cups of halved strawberries, and let cool to room temperature. The sauce can be made up to 24 hours ahead and stored in a covered container in the refrigerator.

To make the biscuits, preheat the oven to 425°F with the rack in the center position. Line a heavy-duty baking sheet with a silicone pan liner, parchment paper, or aluminum foil. Set aside.

In a large mixing bowl, whisk together the flour, salt, baking powder, baking soda, sugar, and dough relaxer, if using. Add the shortening and cut it in with a pastry blender or two knives until the mixture resembles coarse crumbs. Add the buttermilk and heavy cream. Mix with a fork just until the liquids are absorbed.

Turn the dough onto a lightly floured surface and knead gently just until it comes together. Pat the dough into a circle that is ½ to ¾ inch thick. Use a 2½- or 3-inch round cookie or biscuit cutter to cut the dough into 10 biscuits, leaving as few scraps as possible. Gently reroll and cut scraps, if needed. Place the biscuits 1 inch apart on the prepared baking sheet and brush them with the melted butter. Bake for 15 to 20 minutes, until the biscuits are golden brown on top. Transfer the biscuits to a wire rack and let cool for 5 minutes.

While the biscuits are baking, chill a large mixing bowl and beaters that you will use to make the whipped cream. When you are ready to whip the cream, place the cold cream, sugar, and vanilla in the chilled bowl and whip on high speed until thick and the cream holds stiff peaks and looks a bit like mashed potatoes.

Just before serving, split the biscuits and place a biscuit half, cut side up, on each of 10 serving plates. Spoon the strawberry-rhubarb sauce over the biscuits, dividing it evenly, and top with the other biscuit halves and a dollop of whipped cream. Serve immediately.

NOTE: Lora Brody's Dough Relaxer is available at www.lorabrody.com, 888-9-Bakeit; or at the King Arthur Flour Baker's Catalogue, www.kingarthurflour.com, 800-827-6836.

NOTE: Powdered buttermilk, found in the baking section of most supermarkets, eliminates the need to keep fresh buttermilk in the refrigerator. Simply add to your recipe with the dry ingredients the amount of powder specified on the package, then substitute water for the buttermilk called for in the recipe. Store the powdered buttermilk in the refrigerator for up to 1 year.

Index

table of equivalents

* * *

The exact equivalents in the following tables have been rounded for convenience.

LIQUID/DRY MEASURES

U.S.	Metric
¼ teaspoon	1.25 milliliters
½ teaspoon	2.5 milliliters
1 teaspoon	5 milliliters
1 tablespoon (3 teaspoons)	15 milliliters
1 fluid ounce (2 tablespoons)	30 milliliters
¼ cup	60 milliliters
⅓ cup	80 milliliters
½ cup	120 milliliters
1 cup	240 milliliters
1 pint (2 cups)	480 milliliters
1 quart (4 cups, 32 ounces)	960 milliliters
1 gallon (4 quarts)	3.84 liters
1 ounce (by weight)	28 grams
1 pound	454 grams
2.2 pounds	1 kilogram

LENGTH

U.S.	Metric
⅛ inch	3 millimeters
¼ inch	6 millimeters
½ inch	12 millimeters
1 inch	2.5 centimeters

OVEN TEMPERATURE

Fahrenheit	Celsius	Gas
250	120	½
275	140	1
300	150	2
325	160	3
350	180	4
375	190	5
400	200	6
425	220	7
450	230	8
475	240	9
500	260	10